TOXIC
FRIENDS

Also by Susan Shapiro Barash

Little White Lies, Deep Dark Secrets:
The Truth About Why Women Lie

Tripping the Prom Queen: The Truth
About Women and Rivalry

A Passion for More: Wives Reveal the Affairs
That Make or Break Their Marriages

Sisters: Devoted or Divided

The New Wife: The Evolving Role of the American Wife

Second Wives: The Pitfalls and Rewards
of Marrying Widowers and Divorced Men

Mothers-in-Law and Daughters-in-Law: Love,
Hate, Rivalry and Reconciliation

Reclaiming Ourselves: How Women
Dispel a Legacy of Bad Choices

Women of Divorce: Mothers, Daughters,
Stepmothers—The New Triangle

The Men Out There: A Woman's Little Black Book
(with Michele Kasson, Ph.D.)

TOXIC
FRIENDS

*The Antidote for Women
Stuck in Complicated Friendships*

Susan Shapiro Barash

ST. MARTIN'S PRESS ⚹ NEW YORK

In memory of my beloved Aunt Beatty

Author's Note: This book is based on extensive personal interviews with women and experts in the field of psychology and counseling. Names have been changed and recognizable characteristics disguised of all people in this book except the contributing experts. Some characters are composites.

www.stmartins.com

Design by Susan Walsh

Library of Congress Cataloging-in-Publication Data

Barash, Susan Shapiro
    Toxic friends : the antidote for women stuck in complicated friendships / Susan Shapiro Barash. — 1st ed.
        p. cm.
    Includes bibliographical references.
    ISBN 978-0-312-38639-9
    1. Female friendship.   2. Women—Psychology.   I. Title.
    BF575.F66B36   2009
    155.3'33—dc22

                                                            2009016936

First Edition: October 2009

10 9 8 7 6 5 4 3 2 1

CONTENTS

Contents

Men seem to kick friendship around like a football, but it doesn't seem to crack. Women treat it as glass and it goes to pieces.

—Anne Morrow Lindbergh

1. **Please state your age.**

21-30	20 percent
31-40	20 percent
41-50	20 percent
51-60	20 percent
61-70	20 percent

2. **(a) Do you have a best friend?**

Yes	65 percent
No	12 percent
A few	23 percent

   (b) How many years has she been your friend?

0-10	40 percent
11-20	22 percent
21-30	19 percent
31-40	19 percent

3. **(a) Do you ever feel manipulated by your friend?**

Yes	45 percent
No	55 percent

   (b) Have you ever been betrayed by a friend?

Yes	60 percent
No	40 percent

(c) If yes, in what way?

- Stealing husband/boyfriend   54 percent
- Petty issues   14 percent
- Gossip   16 percent
- Career sabotage   16 percent

4. (a) Have you ever had a "toxic friend"?

Yes	55 percent
No	45 percent

(b) Did you stay with the toxic friend or "break up"?

Stayed	25 percent
Broke up	75 percent

(c) If you broke up, what was the main reason?

- Lack of loyalty   13 percent
- Religious reasons   6.5 percent
- Different values   22 percent
- Men   13.5 percent
- Children   16 percent
- Emotional neediness   20 percent
- Money   6.5 percent

5. If you had to describe yourself as a friend, would you say that you are:

(a) someone who leads	20 percent
(b) someone who shares	35 percent
(c) someone who is a pleaser	15 percent
(d) someone who plays different roles with different friends	30 percent

6. (a) Have you ever had a falling-out with a close friend?

Yes	94 percent
No	6 percent

(b) What factors played a role?

• Men	34 percent
• Jealousy	14 percent
• Mothering	7 percent
• Mental illness/ addiction	9 percent
• Different values	27 percent
• Money	9 percent

7. **(a) Have you ever been reunited with a friend?**

Yes	58 percent
No	42 percent

(b) How did this happen?

• Time to forgive	37 percent
• Met again later in life	37 percent
• The Internet	16 percent
• Missed the relationship	10 percent

8. **Have you ever chosen a friend because you believed it would improve your personal situation either in terms of career, children, or social status?**

Yes	40 percent
No	60 percent

9. **Have you ever chosen a friend because you see yourself as "twins," in your lifestyle and/or values?**

Yes	48 percent
No	52 percent

10. **Have you ever felt "tricked" by a friend, drawn in by her appeal only to find out she didn't have your best interests at heart?**

Yes	74 percent
No	26 percent

11. **If you moved far away from a close friend, would you anticipate keeping in touch or that the closeness would lessen?**

Would keep in touch	54 percent
Closeness would lessen	40 percent
Depends upon circumstances	6 percent

12. **Do you believe you would forgive a friend more readily than a husband or boyfriend or a child?**

Yes	22 percent
No	63 percent
Depends upon circumstances	15 percent

13. **Do you find yourself holding on to a female friend even once you know the relationship is no longer working?**

Yes	48 percent
No	52 percent

14. **Do you feel that your mother has been a model for you in terms of your female friends?**

Yes	42 percent
No	49 percent
Somewhat	9 percent

15. **(a) Do you feel competitive or jealous toward women friends?**

Yes	61 percent
No	39 percent

    (b) If so, over what issues?

• Physical appearance	22 percent
• Career	20 percent

- Lifestyle   13 percent
- Men   20 percent
- Children   16 percent
- Money   11 percent

16. Do you feel you are the same kind of friend as an adult woman as you were in high school and college?

Yes   48 percent
No   52 percent

17. Do you ever feel "guilted" into staying friends when you actually don't want to be in the friendship anymore?

Yes   46 percent
No   54 percent

18. Have you ever kept a secret for a friend and lied for her sake?

Yes   53 percent
No   47 percent

(b) If so, what happened?

- It was discovered   14 percent
- It never came out   46 percent
- It was harmless   40 percent

19. Have you ever ended a relationship in a dramatic way?

Yes   34 percent
No   66 percent

20. (a) How would you describe a true friend?

- Honest   16 percent
- Supportive   32 percent
- Loyal   12 percent
- Caring   23 percent
- A good person   7 percent
- Has your best interests at heart   10 percent

(b) Do you believe you have such a friend?

Yes   75 percent
No   25 percent

The Fascination with Our Female Friends

The Greatest Truth

Losing a female friend can have more repercussions for a woman than breaking up with a boyfriend or a husband.

Four Other Truths

✗ Women make more excuses for their female friends than they do for their husbands and children.

✗ Women cite reuniting with an old friend as being among the top five most rewarding experiences.

✗ Women's friendships get "frozen" and don't move forward.

✗ Women confess to hanging on to difficult friendships even when they know they're destructive.

What is it about our women friends that makes the relationships so compelling?

Female friendship is held up to us as an attainable, honorable goal. After all, who understands us better than other women, especially those whom we have let in, in whom we have confided our deepest thoughts and hopes, and with whom we have shared both sorrow and joy? The past forty years have shown us kinship, beginning with the women's movement in the 1960s, when women banded together for the sake of an improved and fairer world for their gender. The belief was underscored by the value of female bonds, and the elements of friendship were enmeshed in female solidarity; the "sisterhood" represented a mutual experience, a covenant. Women supporting women had come to the forefront of a woman's life; the by-product was that female friendships held weight.

As usual, conflicting messages and suppositions for women entered into the equation, creating confusion over what female friendship means and how it is to play out. How much importance are we to allot to our women friends? Women can be mystified by what is expected, although we live in a world where concepts such as "girls' night out," "for women only," and "bachelorette parties" hold special significance. We pursue, praise, and appreciate these relationships while at the same time there is often an underlying sense of uncertainty. We don't always know where a friendship *fits* in the scheme of our lives or what to do with a lost friendship. But what about the friend we stand beside even when she causes more problems than pleasure, flying in the face of *Webster's* definition of a friend, "one attached to another by affection or esteem; a favored companion"?

I have leaned on my closest friends during bad times, celebrated with them on happy occasions, and commiserated with them about the daily grind. I have friends who have carried me through different periods in my life, from high school to college to career, then from marriage to children to divorce and remarriage. At every stage, I've recognized that certain friends come through while others may be unpredictable. And what happens when a friendship is on the rocks and uneasy for both parties? Why aren't we more honest when it comes to making a break with a female friend?

The Changing Face of Female Friendships

The kinds of friendships that women seek today can differ dramatically from those of their mothers' and grandmothers' generations. Baby boomer women describe their grandmothers as women who were not inclined to indulge themselves in such relationships. These women put their days in as mothers and wives (a number of them worked as well), and much of their female companionship was provided by their mothers and sisters. If there were friendships during this time period, they were more common among women of privilege, and still these connections were not the intimate ones of today. In comparison, women of the twenty-first century identify with work friends; our lifestyle invites friendship, despite a hectic pace.

Over the past forty years, female bonding has evolved as the opportunities to engage with our friends have increased. Encouraged by our mothers, teachers, and aunts, we value our female friends, and raise our daughters to do the same, to respect these friends and to expect a great deal from them. We have the luxury of choosing our friends, while obligatory families are, at times, burdensome. Not only are our women friends sought out, but they are available today as never before—via e-mail, text messaging, instant messaging, and cell phones. We have friends for all sorts of reasons, to fill contrasting needs. Implicit is our trust in these friends; we depend upon their opinions and thoughts. In a crisis, large or small, we know exactly who to call. And, more important, there are designated friends to call for specific events, those whom you call for a shopping spree, or to help paint the den, or to pick up a child when you have a scheduling conflict.

Are We Fooling Ourselves?

From kindergarten onward, there is a desire among females to connect with other females. Yet it isn't only the level of devotion to our friends that differentiates women from their male counterparts. There is the emotional component to these friendships, a dependence on the relationship, and a developmental process that differs from the male perspective. An emphasis is placed on loyalty and history, and yet a new friend can suddenly trump a childhood friend, tossing allegiance to the wind. Women seem uncannily capable of such actions.

Nonetheless, female friendship is a meaningful part of my life, as it is for most women. I feel regret for those friends I've lost and gratitude for the ones with whom I've toughed it out. I'll go out of my way to meet a friend, and I look forward to our time together in this pseudo sorority that we have devised. Although we swear by these ties and confide in our women friends as we cannot do with a long-standing male partner, husband, or male friend, our connections are not always free of tension or frustrations. This is the other side to our friendships with women, one that we're often reluctant to face head-on.

Women collect friends because we need them at every stage of our lives, for myriad reasons. I remember when I moved to Connecticut for six years in the 1990s, I made such an effort to stay in touch with my New York City friends and at the same time to develop new friendships in an unknown town. Infiltrating a tight-knit group of women and hoping to be accepted is such a raw memory that it is one reason I decided to embark on this project. Ironically, what women seem to crave most is acceptance among friends, and yet we can be insensitive to the plight of "the new kid in town." What was it exactly that I sought from these women who I hoped would befriend me? It wasn't only companionship, it was the recognition and sense of belonging that friendship yields.

What Is the Standard for Female Friendship?

✗ Is the friend we have to chase down, who doesn't call back or initiate time together, really a friend we want or need?

✗ Are we inclined to dismiss a friend over a superficial matter, let things roll off our backs, or hang on too long to a friendship that is stressful?

✗ What if the friend changes due to a life-altering situation, such as divorce or the death of a loved one?

✗ And what about friends who are competitive, all the while simulating support?

Navigating Difficult Friends

Whatever our mothers felt about their women friends has influenced our own attitudes and reactions to situations. There are those mothers who have shown us an open and respectful approach to female friends, and others who appear too invested, to the exclusion of family members. If a mother has had an unhappy experience with her close friends, this, too, can affect the daughter. Others are jealous or envious of their friends, and teach their daughters to view friends as competitors. Since my book about female rivalry, *Tripping the Prom Queen: The Truth About Women and Rivalry,* delved into this topic, I was aware of the impact of our mothers on our own approach to women in general—female coworkers, sisters, acquaintances, and other mothers whom we know through our children. As several women describe it, a mother's example helps or hinders our own approach to the process.

Ultimately, what we expect of our close female friends and what they expect of us becomes a constant part of our lives. I am keenly aware of which friends have been there in a pinch, and I'm happy to return the favor. I'm also aware of which friend has let me down and the times I've not given enough energy to a friend's problem. This makes me wonder what criteria these relationships are based on and what the expectations are. I know how enthused I've been to meet with a long-lost friend and "pick up just where we left off," or to take a road trip to visit a friend. Yet what about the flip side; what of the tensions that can develop in close friendships when paths have diverged, and perplexity and miscommunication can set in? Have I, too, like some of my friends, leaned on them in hard times and been less accessible when things are status quo?

Women have been watched closely throughout history for their unique and extraordinary friendships. Marie Antoinette's closest cohort and fondest friend, Marie-Louise, princesse de Lamballe, paid dearly for their friendship. Before Marie Antoinette was sent to the guillotine in 1793 for crimes that were never proven, the princesse de Lamballe was killed and her severed head put on a pike and paraded in front of the queen. Catherine the Great poured her heart out in letters to Madame Bielke, and Mary Todd Lincoln's association with Elizabeth Keckley, her seamstress and confidante, raised eyebrows. The two had a falling-out after Lincoln's assassination, when Mrs. Keckley wrote a tell-all book about her White House years. Virginia Woolf and Vita Sackville-West also came from different worlds; Woolf was an egalitarian and Sackville-West an aristocrat. Under the strict social conventions of their time, their closeness was considered uncommon.

Today the media holds sway over how we interpret women as friends, offering examples of successful and failed relationships. The styles of famous friends in film, on television, and in real life have affected our impression of how we are to be. The sugar-coated celebrity friendship is represented by the union of Jennifer Aniston and Courtney Cox Arquette. The cutthroat celebrity friendship is that of Denise Richards and Heather Locklear, whose demise occurred over Richards's now-defunct romance with Locklear's ex. The steadfast celebrity friendship of Oprah Winfrey and Gayle King is exemplary. When women speak of a treasured friend who will go the distance, they draw a comparison to the heroines of the film *Thelma and Louise*. Betty and Veronica of the famed Archie comics have managed to remain best friends and rivals for Archie, while Lucy and Ethel of the 1950s television series *I Love Lucy* were frequent partners in crime.

The Stress of Our Female Friends

A study on female friendships, "Behavioral Responses to Stress: Tend-and-Befriend, Not Fight-or-Flight," conducted in 2000 by psychologists at UCLA, Taylor, Klein et al., reported that women in stressful situations react with a deluge of brain chemicals that *keep* these friendships going. They found that women are reassured when they are with their women friends in times of need, unlike men, who tend to withdraw. Yet women have also told me that what is required by their female friends can be unnerving. Interviewees in big cities and small towns, from various social strata, ethnicities, and age groups, reported high expectations when it comes to female friends, and an impressive list of casualties along the way. What about the surviving friendships; what about the trying times, the *difficult friend*? What are the problems that emerge in these coveted relationships, and how stuck can we be?

The Overrated Connection

Although there has been an influx of books and articles on the rewards of female friendship and how to cope with the loss of a friend who was once close and supportive, there is little talk of the kind of friends women stand by in the face of betrayal, disappointment, and depletion. This kind of friend is someone who pushes our buttons; whose problems, big and small, take up all the oxygen; whose trajectory is exhausting. This friend can be demanding, nosy, aggressive, and she has to have you. Still, many women say that this is the friend who beats the others at winning their time and energy. As women spoke with me about the complexity of particular friendships, several themes became clear.

- ✗ Since there is no road map for our friendships, the boundaries frequently blur and situations become tricky. Women confess to being taken advantage of or, worse yet, taking advantage themselves. Some described feeling "trapped" by a "crazy" friend.
- ✗ Some women feel tied to a close friend when they no longer have something in common. They can either shift gears and remain in the relationship or cut ties—women tend to stay.
- ✗ Women defend those friends who enable them or who are codependent; in this way they perpetuate unhealthy relationships and avoid healthy ones.
- ✗ It isn't that easy for women to make new friends, at any age, and this creates a situation where we tolerate less-than-adequate relationships in order to have friends.

The Deal Breaker

The *New York Times* Modern Love essay "Friendship Too Tight for Breathing Room" by Jessie Sholl, which ran on August 5, 2007, describes a friendship so exclusive that it couldn't survive a romantic interest and reminds us of how women suffer when a friendship sours. Because female friend-ship has similarities to a heterosexual romance, the breakup can be devastating. Monika, 43, who lives in Illinois, felt for-saken by her closest friend during her divorce.

My best friend from grade school decided she wanted to con-tact my ex to say how she'd miss seeing him. Since her link to him had been through me, she called me first to check on how I felt about this, and I said I had to think about it. I decided against it and I told her so. I thought that was the end of it, since she was my child-hood friend. That's why I was so surprised when this friend called my ex anyway. I kept wondering how she had failed to understand my feelings. Or what the draw was—especially when during the mar-riage she hadn't any real contact with him without me. Nor had her boyfriend. I never thought something like this would cause such a break, but since I felt her primary loyalty was to me, we've not spo-ken since.

Compromising Positions

In contrast to Monika is Annabelle, 22, who works in market-ing in New Hampshire. Her relationship with her best friend has become rocky.

I used to think that my best friend was great. Now I look at her in another way. She and I used to be so close—we've been friends since we were ten—but I'm meeting new people and she just doesn't seem as special anymore. I find things about her that bother me, but we'll always be friends because we've been friends for so long. This isn't a friend I'd choose today, but we were together ages ago, and I overlook things for that reason. I don't want any bad feelings, even though we aren't like we used to be when we were together. I tell myself this friendship has to last, no matter that our lives are changing.

Inequalities

If a friendship is not what it once was, as in Annabelle's case, it doesn't have to be the deal breaker of Monika's situation. Women have described their dread at the idea of being without friends, and also fear if a friend becomes less connected. According to a study conducted by Rutter and Garmezy, those of us with friends have a better sense of well-being. Does that make it okay to suffer in these relationships? My interviewees seemed keenly aware of the perks of friendship and the convolutions inherent in the attachment. Nell, 36, a single mother who lives in Michigan, is sensitive to being the needy one.

My friend Angie and I have always trusted each other, but the friendship is more important to me than to her. So I'm the one holding on because I don't want to be without her. She's in the fancier "in" crowd now, and that's hard for me. I used to have a better situation, but now that I'm a single mom, it's not like that anymore. I don't fit in; it's all couples, and I can feel that I'm a fifth wheel sometimes. I'm sure I'm miserable and demanding, but I hang on to her—I refuse to let go. I probably guilt her into being nice, and I know I take advantage, but if I didn't do this, our relationship would disintegrate. I won't let that happen. I feel myself hanging on to her and I weigh the odds and keep on doing it.

Levels of Satisfaction

The nuances and expectations of female friendship are inescapable, as depicted in the television series *Sex and the City*, in which four contrasting women form an impenetrable bond. Despite a few ups and downs, friendship is the most secure part of their lives. In another vein, in *Desperate Housewives*, there is an atmosphere of distrust among women who are supposed to be friends. In *The Golden Girls*, we observe four women in their later years battle it out for the sake of their friendship.

By interviewing two hundred women of assorted backgrounds and ages, I learned how and why women pilot their friendships as they do and what the consequences are. What transpires is influenced by the media, culture, personal experience, and an inherent attachment to female companionship. If a diverse group of women embrace the precept, then the problems and obstacles beneath the surface are all the more disturbing and troubling. According to my research:

- ✗ Over 80 percent of women regretted a breakup with a friend.
- ✗ Sixty-five percent of women said they remain friends with a woman who is difficult on some level.
- ✗ Eighty percent of women said they are competitive with their female friends.
- ✗ Ninety percent of women said their sense of self is tied in to their friendships with other women.
- ✗ Seventy percent of women admitted to spending time thinking about the problems in their friendships.

✗ Eighty-five percent of women said they weren't sure where to place a close friend in terms of priorities.

✗ Over 70 percent of women admitted to power struggles within friendships.

✗ Over 50 percent of women agreed that emotional blackmail exists in their friendships.

The labyrinth of female friendships that causes women to prolong certain alliances that can be so challenging has become part of our everyday lives. The stories I gathered weren't about betrayal and abandonment per se, but about the friendships that endure despite the perils and *why this is so uniquely female.* I wondered if we undervalue or overvalue our female friends, and why the dependency is so much a part of our existence. As my research got under way, I recognized the artifice in positioning our friends. But if we have to choose, where do these friendships fit in? Do female friends come *after* our husbands/boyfriends/lovers, children, parents, and adult siblings in the food chain? Or are they wedged in, at various stages and crisis points? If we can't be without our female friends, and if we look to them to assuage pain, to root for us, to relish our happiness, if a woman's identity is so wrapped up in the friends she makes, it is impossible for these friendships *not* to be consequential.

Shape-Shifting: The Ten Types of Female Friends

As patterns began to emerge among my interviewees, I identified ten styles of friends. I have devoted a chapter to each of these genres, comprised of the leader, the doormat, the sacrificer, the misery lover, the user, the frenemy, the trophy friend, the mirroring friend, the sharer, and the authentic friend. I was curious about the power shifts, both explicit and implicit, between friends, and if women reacted differently to each other in different situations or were always the same kind of friend to every woman. If not, what types of friends more readily adapt, and what provokes this underlying behavior? Although one style can spill into another or we can have characteristics of more than one type of friend, most women with whom I spoke recognized themselves or their friends as fitting into a distinct category and an occasional subcategory.

These styles of friendships have positive components, such as intimacy, affection, and affinity, and negative components, such as competition, duplicity, and disparity. Although we embrace the notion of flawless women friends, we also recognize our friends' shortcomings, and the slippery slope that often evolves appears to be universal. In looking at the intricacies and how affected we are by the twists and turns of these unions, we raise our consciousness. This is in the hope that we will be able to extricate ourselves from harmful friendships, stick with those that have more pros than cons, and come to realize the benefits of the healthy ties we have to our female friends.

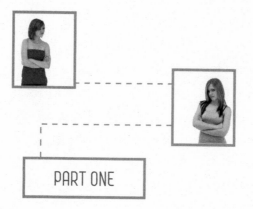

PART ONE

Those We Tolerate:
Romanticizing Our Friends

ONE

The Leader: Ruling the Pack

✗ Does this friend feel more powerful to you than other friends?
✗ Would you go to extremes to be in her good graces?
✗ Do you depend on her plans for your social life?
✗ Does she try to control you at times?
✗ Have you always been attracted to friends who call the shots?

If so, your friend is a leader, and you are part of her "group."

"I'm always in charge; I tell everyone when and where and I decide what's in and what's not," began Eliza, 31, who lives in the Midwest and is a telemarketer. "It sounds easy, but it's a lot of pressure. I don't want anyone else to take my place, but I also find that everyone's social life revolves around me and it's tiring.

"I've been this way since grade school. I remember everyone thinking I was the prettiest and smartest girl by first grade, and everyone wanted to be my friend. It was flattering, but I remember wondering, Wow, what do I do next? I had a boyfriend by fourth grade and he gave me a bracelet. All the other girls were impressed. For years, my birthday party was the big deal in our small town; every girl wanted to be invited. I was picked to be on everyone's team whether it was for a spelling bee in third grade or for a pep rally in high school. By then I was the girl who had a steady boyfriend; the captain of the fire twirlers. This went on in college, too. I guess I know how to be a leader and I'm sort of bossy, because I can be. I definitely make rules. If someone in my group dates a guy I think is a jerk, she starts to doubt him."

What we learn from Eliza is that she not only relishes being a leader, but she also believes in an absolute monarchy—and doesn't seem concerned with her "friends," whom she lords over. She has been at it for so long that it doesn't occur to her that a leader can lose her footing and be replaced. And therein lies the thought process of many a leader—it can be a lot of responsibility leading women around.

The **leader** is the friend we feel we must have, the one who can make or break our social lives. Being the leader renders one a "winner"—she is strong and outspoken; she understands her potency. She is the one who gets us invited to parties and makes the decisions for herself and for her friends. Women of all ages know instinctively that crossing the leader is always a bad idea. She wields influence and control; within groups of friends, she is the lynchpin. This type of friend is familiar to us by high school, as we are reminded in the feature film *Mean Girls* when Rachel McAdams's character, Regina George, pushes the followers of her group, The Plastics, to do her bidding. Her latest prey is Lindsay Lohan's character, Cady Heron, newly arrived on the suburban Chicago scene after having been raised in the African bush by her zoologist parents. Cady's quick assimilation into the fast lane and a fight for the role of leader ensue.

The Slippery Slope

Since leadership has eluded women in our society for centuries, it makes sense that "the leader" among women friends is a title that is not easy to attain or sustain. A leader in a group of friends may have traits that reflect those of a female leader in government or in the workplace. After all, it's a rough climb to the top, with obstacles at every turn and harsh judgments for those women who desire to lead in any arena. However, a group of friends is singular in its mission, comprised of several or more females who seek one another out for companionship and connection. A leader, more than other types of female friends, views her role as a job that she hopes is manageable, without foul play among the ranks. Women feel rewarded for belonging to a clique or a clan; this social support offers security and assuages loneliness.

As we mature, the longing to be a part of a group persists, as does the leader's ability to assign us roles. The leader identity, minus the high school mentality of *Mean Girls,* is apparent in the HBO series *Big Love.* This drama about a seemingly righteous man who is also a polygamist with three wives (called "sister-wives") and three sets of children features Jeanne Tripplehorn as Barb, the first (and only legal) wife, who leads the other two, Nicky, the second wife (played by Chloë Sevigny), and the third, youngest wife, Margene (played by Ginnifer Goodwin). What is so fascinating is how the two younger wives manipulate each other; they're cloying and incisive. But these women also genuinely yearn for a connection to each other and for Tripplehorn's character, Barb, to lead. Even when the leader annoys us or exerts too much dominion, we are drawn to her.

Inner Sanctum

You've worked hard to cultivate your assemblage of friends these past fifteen years since college, and you've been the ring-leader. The dynamic has changed over time, and not everyone's lives are parallel anymore. There are those who are married with children—some of these mothers are working and some are not—others are preoccupied with their careers, and some friends are getting divorced. In this diverse group, what holds everyone together is devotion and reliance. In fact, when articles on toxic friends and breakups among women run in women's magazines, you thank your lucky stars this isn't part of your life.

That is, until recently, when you invited a new "member" into the group, and it stirred up a few problems. It seemed the right thing to do, although without your reaching out to her, she wouldn't have stood a chance. It now seems she's become divisive and is excluding you. This woman has invited the others in the "group" to her home, and you haven't been invited, and it's come back to you that she's said a few unkind things. The worst part is that you consider her a friend. And she's so charming that no one would believe she was trying to exclude you anyway. You decide to buck up and try harder to win her over.

Narcissistic Tendencies

The above example shows us how a woman who has worked hard to be the leader is exposed to a withering of command. This has been reflected in television shows, quite often as of late. In the reality television series *The Girls Next Door*, Hugh Hefner and his three girlfriends show us something identifiable and titillating about women befriending one another in a select group and competing at once. Holly is the leader, representing Hefner's "wife" of the three. Despite Holly's rank, she's still willing to scheme and undermine the others. This proves that one's role as leader is frequently precarious and always highly touted. In the 2007/2008 season of *Desperate Housewives,* actresses Marcia Cross and Dana Delaney (new to the 2007 season) had "their claws out for each other," as reported in *Star* magazine. Apparently, Cross and Delaney bickered "on-screen" and off, and in true form for those with a leader mentality, over which actress has more screen time.

The Crowd Pleaser

When we consider the leader's desire for recognition, to be the outstanding one in the crowd, we have to ask if her influence over her friends is pure. In a culture in which the individual is recognized for her talents and thoughts, groups of friends are, nonetheless, often formed based on shared attitudes and belief systems. Even if the leader stands apart from the group by definition, she represents a collective point of view. If a group of young women decides to boycott the prom, the leader is at the head of the opposition. If someone is going to be singled out, the leader determines who she is and how she will be treated; when a new "member" is allowed in, the leader orchestrates this change in the ranks. If this all sounds sophomoric and callow, consider Janine, 37, who lives in Santa Fe, where she is a chef and the self-proclaimed leader of her social circle. She described her leverage and how if she alters her behavior, her friends will do the same.

Anything that's social for me is about my being ahead of my friends and having a kind of attitude. I don't want just one friend; I want at least four or five women, who have to be at any event *after* me. These are my closest friends and I want them to think they're missing out on something if we don't do things together. At times I've encouraged these friends to be unfriendly to other women, and no one can bring a new friend in. It works best this way. Since I'm a chef, we'll meet at the restaurant where I work and we'll decide what happens that season; if we're going to go to every party in town, if we're going to buy theater tickets ... If someone seems to have a lot of ideas, I'm wary. We also have to tell one another what's going on, offer support if someone is going through a tough time or getting divorced or breaking up with a boyfriend.

In Janine's experience we see a very deliberate manner regarding her place as leader. This identity is a large part of her life, and needing friends appears to be about enhancing her position. Little is mentioned about how her friends mold her perspective, but much concern is expressed for her status.

Part of the Herd

When leaders describe the benefits of their stance, many times they omit the essentials of friendship: concern, caring, and intimacy. These qualities are not always at the forefront of the leader's commitment to her friends—she is too busy keeping her position intact and leading the herd. As Dr. Claire Owen, psychology professor at Marymount Manhattan College, points out, superiority is a part of the interaction among friends. "When a woman has been taught to reach for her own individual best, it can be complicated, and unfortunately, this might not always be positive for her friends."

Consider Deana, 34, who works full-time in television and lives in a city in the Northeast. Although the leader among her group of friends might be annoying, she also takes care of Deana's social life.

I admit, where would I be without her? She is the one who gets me going, and it adds something to my life to meet her and our friends on these appointed dates. We've been doing this for years, and I'd say this friend is almost a facilitator. I end up not thinking for myself, or wondering where I'll go on holidays—it's all taken care of, and with my busy schedule at work, that's fine. She's the common denominator, and she also has the advantage of planning what she wants. I'm lucky I can afford what she plans; some of our friends actually can't. Then she has to shuffle around some, but this friend tends to stay with her plan, and if you're strapped, you bail out. I wouldn't want to be her, but I'm grateful every Christmas and lonely New Year's that there's someone like her, who puts it all together, bossy as she is.

The Disciples: Drawn to the Leader

In the following chapters we will observe how deeply other types of female friends are affected by the leader, particularly the sacrificer, the mirroring friend, the user, and the trophy friend. A woman sought by the leader might discover that this aspect of female bonding is ephemeral and depends upon what the leader's priority is. For instance, if the leader is planning a bowling night and you are the only one of her devotees who bowls, she will focus on you for your expertise (thus she is also a user to a degree). As many of my interviewees described it, one day a woman feels chosen by the leader, but when her favor turns to another, it can be disheartening and incomprehensible. The leader may also have her cohort, her closest friend, and beyond this, her members. And there are those leaders who are sensitive to each woman's needs, and they are appreciated for this.

Leadership Qualities
- ✗ Earning the trust of the group
- ✗ Being honest with your friends/followers
- ✗ Adapting to the changing requirements of the members
- ✗ Being in tune with each friend's feelings

versus

Leadership at Risk
- ✗ The leader puts her needs ahead of her friends' needs
- ✗ She is willing to lie to get ahead

✗ She hangs on tightly to her original take on things
✗ She is a user or a trophy friend

While women are aware that the leader achieves her title through social currency, popularity, and personality, this doesn't affect their desire to belong to her club. The leader is usually outspoken and has a take-charge attitude; she might feel entitled as well. Women know this and accept the trade-off as the "price" of enrollment. The leader surrounds herself with assorted types, who do not always reflect her characteristics. Consider Avery, 49, who described being the best friend to a leader as a chancy business. She lives in a Southern city, where she works at an architectural firm.

My friend, who is always in charge and practically blows a whistle, takes us all to Arizona for a road trip each year. At first I'm quiet and say very little, just go with the flow. But these women aren't really my friends; I only go because she organizes it and invites me and because she and I are so close. By now I know what to expect, and we've become her group—not our group, but hers. I'm not the one to put something like this together, to walk into every hotel and museum ahead of everyone else and to pick which store we should shop in and what kind of clothes to find. Still, in my job I'm competitive and I've done well; I'm no shrinking violet.

So I end up getting sort of stubborn as these trips go on—even though I go every year and I always am up for it in the beginning. I drag behind and stay quiet the first week, but by the second week, I get obstinate, and I stop being so easygoing and sharing this and that: my sweatshirt, my books, my CDs. I see this pattern—I start off so that anyone can borrow my pashmina, but after a while, I hate anyone who does. I get resistant. But I don't turn her down when she invites me anywhere; she's one of my best friends.

Em, 27, who is the mother of three and works part-time as a nurse in a Southern town, takes another approach to her relationship with her friend who is in command. Em's view is that her friend does whatever it takes to protect her role, and it has been this way since high school.

I'm someone who gets along with everyone, but my one friend, since we were 12 years old, always wants to be the important one. When we were younger it worked, and she made us all afraid enough to look up to her. But I don't get how she can be that way now, when she'll lie and cancel plans or not even show up. She's like this now because the rest of us in the group are mothers and she doesn't have kids and I think she's worried about it. This brings out the worst in her. We're all Hispanic and it's part of our culture to marry early and have kids young. Some of us split with our husbands—it's more common than not having been married yet, like this friend. I've been with my husband for ten years, and that's a long time. This friend doesn't like that, either; no one else in our group has been married this long, and she thinks I'm showing off. Her attitude is that she's supposed to set the rules, so I don't tell her as much as the others—I say more to the friends who have kids too.

If this friend could be more honest with me and the rest of the group, if she didn't seem jealous, if she could level with me and face her feelings, we'd all be better off. I stopped calling her for a while, and still she didn't face how she acts. The others also try to avoid her, and then we feel pressured to see her. She doesn't say a word; she acts like none of this is happening, as if things are like they were ages ago.

When Em speaks of the leader as someone who lies and won't level with her, she's describing a woman in denial. While most leaders with whom I spoke for this chapter were keenly aware of their obligations and the image they present to their core group, Em's friend doesn't conduct herself in this manner. Instead, she sounds ungrounded; it's little wonder the women are distancing themselves and her supervision is waning. In "Denial Makes the World Go Round," an article that ran in *The New York Times* on November 20, 2007, Benedict Carey described "willful blindness," a form of denial in which "the person keeps the topic off limits, perhaps even to himself." Carey wrote that the use of denial in our interactions with others is both "potentially destructive" and "also critically important to nourishing close relationships." Apparently, denial began as a defense against "early humans' hypersensitivity to violations of trust." This applied to "small kin groups," in which falsehoods could result in a real danger to members. When we consider how life revolves around the leader, Em's frustration with her friend, who is not only irresponsible but also denies that she is insensitive, is understandable.

The Scenario for Leaders

According to a study by Cheng, Bond, and Chan, women are more intimate with their friends and more willing to share their feelings than are male friends and acquaintances. While this is a familiar concept, what is interesting to note is how a close circle of female friends operates unlike paired friendships. Often enough within these factions, there are issues of competition and self-confidence, a caste system and subgroups. In listening to women for this chapter, I learned that the initial link for women in a clique or a clan is most frequently a shared lifestyle (more on this in Chapter 8, "The Mirroring Friend"). Hence, when the commonality is no longer there, the group may dissipate of its own accord, and because groups are appealing, the members will find new groups to support their latest interests. For the leader, this may be disconcerting. She would prefer to keep the group intact rather than to find or create another in order to rise to leader once again.

The Leader Is Not Invested in Self-Disclosure

Being in the shoes of the leader isn't always as satisfying as it appears to the other types of women who form the clique. While she is set apart from the herd mentality, she is also responsible for her group, for their attitude toward one another and toward those outside the group. In the classic late-nineteenth-century ballet *Swan Lake,* Prince Siegfried falls in love with Odette, who is a swan by day and a young woman at night, the result of a spell cast upon her by an evil sorcerer. When Odette leads the other swan-maidens (also prisoners of the sorcerer) in a dance, it ends tragically for her, and her demise rattles the swan-maidens. Thus, what affects the leader affects the followers. In today's world, there are several common scenarios:

Our Mother's Influence. As is almost always the case, our mother's example has a penetrating effect upon how we are to our friends. If she was a front-runner among her friends, the daughter may follow in her footsteps. If a mother was more reticent, the daughter might rebel and be outspoken, or she might be the quiet type too.

Chrysalis to Butterfly. Morphing into a leader is possible after a personal experience or epiphany. For example, someone with newfound power can become the leader and change the dynamic of the group. She may even attract new members.

A Heavy Load. Enough leaders become exhausted, whether they are good or bad leaders. Since being a leader is exalted, it can be secretly burdensome. As one leader explains it, "I take charge, whether it's getting tickets to a concert or organizing a shopping excursion. I never get a break."

Varied Expectations. Not all leaders are the same. Some merely stage their friendships for the sake of the recognition they gain. Others are truly invested in the friendships and desirous of the results of these connections.

The Wizard of Oz. Dorothy had the charisma to bring people together for a common cause. Although she led several men down the yellow brick road, this leadership quality would have applied to women as well (if any had been around). Women feel it is almost a calling to organize and gather their friends.

Tribal Friendships

In Rebecca Wells's Southern tale *Divine Secrets of the Ya-Ya Sisterhood,* we realize how deeply etched is the role of each woman in a group of friends that has spanned forty years. The pronounced leader is Vivi, who is dramatic and vivacious, and was the beauty of the Ya-Ya's when they were younger. Vivi's secret and sadness is contained in the sisterhood, as the members buoy one another and absorb one another's triumphs and losses over the years, bonded by their deep roots to the South and their common values. Women with whom I spoke described a similar attachment to their group of friends; again, this is predicated upon the tone of the leader. The theory of homogamy, finding an eligible partner based on similar race, age, education, social class, and religion, which applies to marriage, can apply to female friendships as well, particularly in clans. Although one would assume that less conflict would occur in these friendships built on familiarity, this is not always the case.

In large cities and small towns alike, women detail their attachment to their group and the leader's significance therein. Various factors can inspire groups to form.

Society and Money

Darcy, 48, who is an attorney practicing in Washington, D.C., believes she is a leader among women in terms of lifestyle and accomplishments.

The common thread is that we're all driven and successful, and we live that life. Our friendship is crisis proof because there's a sense of loyalty and understanding. At least, from my perspective, since I'm the one everyone listens to and who makes all the plans. Definitely we have this need to be intellectually exciting.

And we talk about the real story; I don't want to hear how everyone's life is so perfect and there are no struggles. So we talk about how hard it is to have kids and jobs. Some of us have husbands too. We talk about how hard-earned our degrees are and how hard our jobs are. We all want this, that's the thing—no one wants a boring life.

Although Darcy defines her followers as being bound by their ambition, Leslie, 41, who lives in a Midwestern city where she is a full-time "socialite," has purposely chosen this route.

My friends and I go to lunch a few times a week. We try not to gossip, and if anyone has a problem, we're supportive, but mostly we are fairly closed about our personal lives. I buy tickets to charity events, and I'm interested in both the arts and in raising funds for medical research. I knew for years that I wanted this instead of a career, and none of my friends work; it's not what we do. I end up being in charge because I put tables together and do so much charity work. I don't know that I aspired to this, but I admit I never wanted the stresses of working outside the home. I know some women might look at this and say we're frivolous, but it's work, raising money for causes and getting your friends together in a way that everyone is happy.

Motherhood as the Link

Grace, 34, who is a working mother of three and lives in Southern California, is beginning to doubt that she can suit the needs of her coterie.

I have pockets of different friends, and I play different roles within them. I'm involved with a book club with the mothers in my neighborhood, and I consider these women my friends. All our kids go to the same school, and in the beginning, I was the organizer and had the qualities of being a leader, because I'm witty and solid. Things were fine until I made a decision about my girls that didn't fit with the attitudes around here. Then I lost some friends, if they ever *were* friends.

But as a working mother I have my own ideas about raising children, and I've allowed my daughters to come home from school alone. Even the working mothers find this horrifying, although they're intrigued. So when I announced that there's too much hovering, I was no longer popular and lost any leadership role I might have had. One mother even commented that I'm never at the school and don't know what's going on. I realize how being a leader means the other mothers, who might or might not actually be your friends, have to approve every step you make, and I'm too independent to be that way.

What Grace's story drives home is the fact that among working mothers as well as nonworking mothers, there is a code and expectations; when she broke a "rule," it was met with dissension. This is serious enough for Grace to feel that her leadership is in jeopardy and that her membership itself is threatened since she no longer echoes her friends/fellow mothers' point of view concerning child rearing. In such instances, it is a common goal that defines the friendships, rather than friends congregating because they are drawn to one another as individuals.

Comfort Levels: Single Women

As reported by the U.S. Census, 53.5 million women in America are single, consisting of those who are divorced, those who never married, and those who are widowed. Each of these populations has an individual identity and a distinct impression of how the world views them. Hence, a leader among these subgroups is valuable, despite changing social attitudes of the past forty years toward women who are without long-standing partners or husbands. Women who fall into these categories have described a residual defensiveness, since the bias against single women has dissipated but still exists today. When *The Mary Tyler Moore Show* debuted in 1970, Moore's character, Mary Richards, a single woman who was neither divorced nor widowed and who evolved into a career woman, represented a new slice of life for American women.

Natalie, 44, who is an office administrator and lives in a Northeastern city, described how her singlehood was telling in terms of her place as a leader.

During my divorce, I really found out who my friends were. I had a fairly comfortable life before my husband and I split. I was sort of a social queen, someone who had parties and entertained. I watched it all slip away, and it was upsetting, but there was nothing to do. So I got a job and became realistic. I was dropped by some women, and one of my closest friends became the new leader. I doubt I'll ever have that kind of life again, and I won't have one group of friends like I had when we were all married and living the same lifestyle.

I decided to be smart about this. Now I'm with women who are also divorced—women from my gym and from my office—and we've all got battle wounds and we have a leader. I listen to her because she's the prettiest and gets boyfriends, and being her friend is worthwhile. I couldn't be a leader here; it's all foreign to me. I'm happy to follow, especially having been the go-to person in my own time. This divorced world is so different from the married world, and she's a survivor, so she gives me hope.

While Natalie is content to relinquish her once-cherished position as leader, she is also someone who appreciates a new leader in her new stage of life. For Mary, 37, who is a single mother of two and lives in a rural area, where she works as a massage therapist, a woman's support group has given her the opportunity to become a leader.

I was on Xanax after my husband died, but I pulled it together when I met other widows and divorcées at a local church. Some of these women had been wallowing in their misery for months, for years. When I got there, I was the one who was more collected. I thought we should pass around any single, discarded men, and it was very successful. Everyone had a sense of humor; we kept a chart. If someone had ended up with a real love affair, it might have shaken things up. But it didn't happen, and that sort of bonded us together too, the idea that every guy was worth a few dates and that was it. It's more a game and we're all in it—it makes us a group.

Eventually I didn't have to be medicated to get through the days. Instead I concentrated on my new friends. I'm the one who gets us all together, plans dinners and spa days. One of the women is a whiner and one is spoiled; one is all about money. But they all seem to like that I'm here, planning what's next.

What is notable about Mary's attitude and involvement with her followers is how much she relishes the opportunity to be held in esteem. Although her friends are younger women, her interview brings to mind the television series *The Golden Girls,* which ran on NBC from 1985 until 1992. This comedy that followed the antics of four older women garnered the attention of the American public and, in terms of female friendship, exemplified the struggles that ensue when several types of women are united. Starring Bea Arthur as the leader, Dorothy, a strong-willed, amusing character who could be slightly mean-spirited at times, it also featured Betty White as Rose, the vulnerable blonde; Rue McClanahan as Blanche, who is sex starved and egotistical; and Estelle Getty as Sophia, Dorothy's mother, an annoying woman who sometimes schemes to get her way.

The Hierarchy of Working Women

What women in business and politics have in common is the dearth of females in their position and, in enough situations, a lack of support from other women. Only ten women have run Fortune 500 companies (including such notable women as Meg Whitman, former CEO of eBay; Andrea Jung, CEO of Avon; and Claire Babrowski of RadioShack), and this, of course, is the problem. The road to such achievement for women is arduous, and one wonders if early experiences as a leader among friends impacts their later success. Although we know that Oprah Winfrey's best friend is Gayle King, beyond this, not much information is to be gleaned concerning powerful women and their friends and how those relationships mix with their careers. Everyday women, however, who are immersed in their careers speak of female friends as having to "fit" with their finely honed lives. These women also describe themselves as leaders by nature. Consider Lauren, 35, who works as a finance manager and lives in a rural area. Married with three children, Lauren feels that her work life is entwined with her personal life.

I'm the boss of five women, and we're also friends. We work in a very corporate structure and spend time together after work as an extension of our day. Work is the way we relate, and I can't really identify with women outside my work world. Sometimes there are subtle jealousies, but mostly it's a group that I put together and keep together. We hang out, and I'm the one who is the peacemaker and also the one they sort of look up to. I have kids and no one else does, and I've supervised these women at work for the past few years. I doubt we'd be together if it wasn't for our careers, but we are and it's a big part of our lives. I can see how there could be some petty fights or backbiting, and I won't have it. It's really against my rules, and this all feels familiar to me. I was like this back in college, when I was in a sorority, and I'm like this with my own sisters.

I'd say I'm the leader in my work crowd by choice—no one else seems to have the time. When I'm off work, I know the stay-at-home mothers are a tight-knit crowd and I avoid them; I stick with what I know. My life outside my family revolves around work, and that's where I'm the leader. I've always been the the organizer among my friends, the one who makes the decisions. I don't know if I'm genuinely liked, but I'm genuinely respected.

Lauren described herself as a referee who gets some positive results. In contrast, Suzanne, 33, who is an attorney in a Southern city, admitted she spends time feeling uneasy with her work friends and views herself as a follower, not a leader.

I'd rather stay with this handful of women lawyers than walk away and be relieved of their company but nervous about where I stand. I don't trust the woman who heads up the office and is a kind of social director too—she makes me so unhappy. So I put up a front that I'm ready for anything and that I look forward to social events. She knows I'm a hard worker, so this is about the other part, where it's obligatory and supposed to be about friendship. That includes when we go for drinks or holiday parties. I wouldn't cross her, and would always befriend her because it's work. But I know I don't have any feelings for her and I'm operating out of fear. I just do what she suggests socially and workwise, and I feel that this way, I'm keeping my job.

In my personal life, I wouldn't tolerate this, and I'm more of a loner. I have stayed clear of cliques and clans because they never work for me. What's so ironic is that it's right there, every day, at my office, where I have no option.

Posing as Friends

As we have witnessed throughout this chapter, the friend who is the leader has a moral responsibility to those she leads. Yet in realizing the plight of both Lauren, as the leader, and Suzanne, as the follower, we see an intimidation factor based on prestige, acceptance, and need. In this way, some groups of female friends become an adult playing field for bullying and fear tactics, orchestrated by the leader of the pack.

Bullying and Conquering

But what about the female in a powerful position who is friendless and a bully? This unsettling alternative is shown to us in the feature film *Michael Clayton*, in which Tilda Swinton plays Karen Crowder, a heartless litigator for U-North, which is fighting a class action suit. Swinton's character's career depends upon a victory, while George Clooney's character, Michael Clayton, is a "fixer" at the firm that believes they will win the case. As I watched Karen Crowder epitomizing the female loner whose pure ambition and aggression careen her forward (she is willing to lie, cheat, kill, and bribe to sustain her position), she seemed rudderless, yet, until the end, strong somehow. Michael Clayton, in contrast, is surrounded by family and friends, at work and outside of work, albeit a flawed bunch. But does Swinton's character have to be so tainted by the system, to be virtually without one woman in her life *and* without scruples? Is the message that women in power do not get a constituency but go it alone? What does this say about the corporate world and a woman's place in it? Might we have pitied this character had she had a group of female coworkers whom she solicited for help with her plan, rather than operating so independently?

Whether a leader is trustworthy or not, either way, she is in the driver's seat and has to have followers. If an aggressive female can create insecurity among the other women, she nonetheless requires the other women and, to this end, might play them against one another. As Rachel Simmons writes of female aggression in her book *Odd Girl Out*, "alternative aggression" begins when girls in school bully one another, and has a direct consequence on one's self-esteem that can last into adulthood. Dr. Ronnie Burak, a psychologist, notes that a leader who utilizes a fear factor is resorting to an immature behavior of "watching your back," reminiscent of adolescence. "Women can be very disturbed about the workplace or about other mothers at school or about old friends, and how one woman in particular rules the roost. When you make yourself feel better by making the members feel worse, it's counterproductive and cruel," she remarks.

Antoinette, 47, who lives in upstate New York, where she runs a division of the company she works for, has developed a practical approach.

I'm fully aware of what goes on, but this is a work environment, not the Girl Scouts. When there is backbiting or the women in my group aren't being kind to one another, I stop it at once. I'm aware of my position at all times, and I know I'm respected, if not beloved. But I have a business to run, and I can't be sidetracked by what happens among the women. I try to be everyone's friend and I try to show that I care for all of my staff. We have to be friendly since we have no time for any friends outside of work. On the other hand, this isn't a touchy-feely atmosphere. If there were no women here, I'd be as focused and ready for success as I am with the women who are hired. I'm in charge—they call me "General" and I don't mind. If I see that something isn't working, I call it out. I do put myself first, but I'm also aware of my obligation to the other women in the company, and I want to be more than a boss, if it works.

Heading the Pack

If the leader describes a lifelong complexity in her role among her friends, those who follow may realize that being part of a female chain of command can limit their options. Friendship itself is defined broadly as it applies to a leader, since women often congregate based on a mutual need, as exemplified in Natalie's interview. Simultaneously, we have the determination of some leaders to always be in charge, as expressed by Eliza, to the point where friendship seems secondary to the position. For those of us who shadow the leader, Em's experience is the one that resonates. Their stories remind us of how multilayered the system is for the leader/follower.

What Models Do We Have?

While being a leader is heady stuff, leaders themselves can be insecure and weighed down by the position. However, few are ready to relinquish the prestige, and as reported, some women are at it their entire lives, shifting into whatever kind of leadership role each stage demands. Renata, 62, who lives in West Virginia, has had the same friend as queen bee since they were in their early twenties. Twenty years ago, Renata "defected."

I had this friend who told all of us in our hometown what to do. For years we all listened. We listened when the kids were small and she thought the girls should take ballet classes. And when the kids were older she told us the boys should learn chess. She told us all how to run our lives and what shows to see when we traveled to

New York, where to shop and where to eat. Finally, when I was about 40, I realized I didn't want her advice or to have her running my life. All of my friends flocked to her, and whatever she suggested or whatever arrangements she made for all of us seemed fine. Not to me. I wanted to be independent, so I pulled away. I felt her distance, and the others all treated me with the same distance, acting like her. I didn't care; I wanted to make my own plans and my own decisions.

Led Astray

There are those leaders who can coax their followers into thinking in a specific way. Or the women identify so closely with a particular group that everyone mimics the attitude of the leader. For instance, Samantha, 37, who lives in a suburb of an Eastern city and is married with two children, regards her group of stay-at-home mothers as admittedly "clannish" and unfriendly toward working mothers.

Maybe it's my ego, but I have always been the one taking charge. I do it now through mothers I know. I've chosen not to work, and I want women who have made the same decision to feel good about themselves. I've always enjoyed seeing people rewarded by my plans, and now it's the mothers in my neighborhood. We have a lot to focus on. I feel like I'm taking these women to another level, looking at our roles in a way they might not have done on their own. I think of it as a job, and these women sort of work for me. I was a leader in high school; I was a leader in college and with my friends when we were first married, before we had kids. My mother was a leader, and that helps, plus I've had all this practice.

Samantha admitted that she has convinced some of her "followers" to be unfriendly toward the working mothers.

What makes being a leader of nonworking mothers a bit differ-ent is that we're always aware of the other group, the working mothers. So as mothers we're divided, and that's fine. I think it's okay to be so involved that you see the working mothers as adver-sarial. I believe in what we stand for.

Corrine, 42, who lives in New Jersey, belongs to a group of women that has opposed a neighbor's addition to her home.

First of all, there are only women involved with this issue that has to do with our town—and I'm not sure why that is. Then, the women have become enemies over it, because one set is against the addition and the other is in favor of it. In each group, everyone is close now, joined over disagreeing with the other group. I think the women in charge believe they're running for office. It's gotten so ugly and out of control. I actually wonder why I'm even doing this; it reminds me of high school.

Leaders Versus One-on-One Friendships

Interviewing women about being the leader of a group or a clique raises questions that do not apply to one-on-one friend-ships. The friends/followers have high expectations of the leader when it comes to understanding and decision making. Women not only have larger groups of friends than do men but are also more affected by any negative occurrence within their clique. A study by Cunningham and Barbee points out the signifi-cance of "perceived support," meaning if a woman believes that she has assistance from her friend, whether this is the case or not, it improves her health and provides a sense of belonging. The climate of any group of friends is determined by the leader and her followers combined. While Julia, 45, who works in public relations and lives out west, realizes it would be easier to lead if her friends were more amenable, she also savors the post.

I'm primed to run everyone's life, and my friends usually love it. I throw the parties, I pick up their kids at religious school and take them somewhere fun to reward them, I have all the ideas. How can it be that I'm also the one who works full-time? To top it off, there's one friend in the group who drains me, and it's not that I don't stand on my head for her. I have to—it's my job, the one I signed up for, to look after everyone. She's just miserable, and until she gets a new husband or a raise, it isn't going to improve. So I keep her happy and I'm exhausted. Then I remind myself I'm the one; I'm the sergeant in this army.

The Skinny on Leaders and Followers

As the experts quoted in this chapter note, negative leadership can be intimidating and counterproductive, yet women often seek out a group with a leader nonetheless and will make excuses in order to belong. It comes as little surprise that 60 percent of the women with whom I spoke for this chapter were pleased with their position of strength as the leader. In comparison, 40 percent of followers felt they had a well-balanced attitude in belonging to their group, and that being the leader wasn't something to which they aspired. Of the followers, 40 percent were reluctant to leave a group despite their discomfort with the leader's style, and 40 percent reported a dependency upon their leader. Only 20 percent were willing to leave the leader and forfeit the friendship.

In such situations, we have to ask ourselves the salient questions:

Do you and your friends spend too much time trying to please the leader?

For some women in the group, it will be easier than for others to be in synch with the leader. If it doesn't work for you, it's time to reconsider what this relationship means to you.

Are you secretly relieved when the leader has the flu?

If your leader is intimidating, it's time to rethink why you are her friend and a member of the group. If you are pandering to her and it makes you uneasy (enough that you're actually happy she's sick), it's time to stop.

Do you suspect the leader of being less than fair or genuine?

Close to 70 percent of my interviewees did not care about the leader's attitude as long as they were included. But if your friend is the leader and you are in the 30 percent who do care, it is wise to rethink the relationship and perhaps discuss this with her.

Does your leader feel competitive toward another group of women?

Forty percent of followers said that their leader and group of friends were rivalrous toward another faction of women. If this is not comfortable for you, it's worth considering another group that better reflects your philosophy.

Is the leader a winner in a way that appeals to you?

If the leader offers a positive experience, then it's a good idea to stay in her group and enjoy the merits of belonging. When women who seek a coterie of women admire the leader, there is a high level of contentment.

TWO

The Doormat: High School Onward

✗ Does your friend soothe you when you're down?

✗ Does she avoid any drama or tension?

✗ Does she seem to have little identity of her own?

✗ Do you wonder if she ever tires of her "poor me" mode?

✗ Does she sympathize with your problems and always take your side?

If this is the case, your friend is a doormat who wipes up your troubles.

"I've always been attracted to friends with problems. I chose this type when I was young and it's been that way my whole life," said Nell, 39, who lives in Nevada, where she teaches yoga. "It's meatier to have friends like this; it's what life is all about. I know how to find these friends, and I wouldn't pick any other kind. I don't want sunny, happy-go-lucky people in my life. My closest friends tell me their sad stories and call at all hours. I've always liked being the friend who is there for them and listens for days. If I'm with someone and her life is upbeat and easy, I'm not interested. I don't have much to say to her and not much about her is appealing. And I don't really believe it's the case anyway, so it means we're in a superficial relationship.

"I'm looking for friends who have turmoil and obstacles to overcome. I think I make sense and I'm rational when I comfort them. That's because it's not my issue but theirs, and that's rewarding. I don't say too much about myself unless it's my turn with something wrong, but even then, I'm more likely to keep it to myself. I find these friends, ones who have all this going on, and then help them by listening, and calming them down. Sometimes I advise, but not so much. It's really about me feeling like I'll be there for them."

The **doormat** is a martyr, and the position she takes among her friends is obvious: She isn't one to make her demands known and rarely questions anything. The leader finds her very accommodating, but following a leader isn't the doormat's only function. She is also useful when any friend, in any category, is in a bad way—the doormat absorbs her sorrows willingly. The doormat yearns to belong to a group, and also seeks out intimate friendships. To this end, she isn't critical and won't give you a hard time. She might be so desperate for friendship that she'll indulge the friend who shops too much, the party girl, the gym rat, the brokenhearted; she's very true to her part.

The friend is more likely to be the recipient of her friend's troubles than to divulge her own, as Nell described. But when the doormat has suffered too, her empathy is at an all-time high. For example, a doormat whose fiancé has broken up with her will be more than merely sympathetic to her friend who is now enduring the same situation—she'll be a second skin. We stick with the doormat because she's hard to resist and she is refreshingly steady. Several interviewees remarked that they wished their sister and/or mother was more doormat-like; this friend fills the void.

Wiping It Clean

For many women, blotting the anguish of others is a knee-jerk reaction; the social conditioning of women has made this a habitual and easy air to assume. After all, it worked for us in grade school; by high school the typecasting of girlfriends is set, and the tolerance level of an understanding friend is welcomed. Having a doormat as a friend early on makes it hard to be without one later, when same-sex friendships are so ingrained and life becomes knottier. Being a doormat when young can have perks too, and some have welcomed the chance. As Katherine Taylor wrote in her essay "Girls, Mean and Otherwise," which appeared in *The New York Times* on September 16, 2007, it was enthralling to make friends at boarding school in the late 1980s, and to observe her elegant friend's existence. Taylor described herself as educable and willing to assimilate when she came from Fresno, California, to New York City to visit this friend at 17. "I learned how to half smile when I wanted to laugh out loud, how to feign ease at parties full of worldly strangers, how to conceal my own drunkenness," she wrote. Taylor lamented that she lost touch with this friend, who knew the nuances of sophistication as only someone who grows up in the midst of it can, and that this friend "didn't teach [her] enough."

Those who are doormats say it's appealing to meet women who will spill the goods *and* might rely on you as well. If not, doormats would struggle to justify their place in the network of female friends. Nell might view herself as a sort of savior, but her radar for friends with quandaries makes it satisfying, and she feels this is her niche. In contrast, Judith, 45, who sells real estate in a small Southern town, seems to be saturated with one of her close friends.

I have this friend who was always trouble and she still is. Our friendship was based on my willingness to listen, ever since we went to Sunday school together. Recently this friend got divorced and moved away. Now we write long e-mails and it's always the same; I'm the hole she fills with her troubles. I don't like the way the friendship works, with me telling her how to fix her life all the time. Not that she listens; it's more that I just have to be the sounding board. I rarely get to express my feelings, and she doesn't want to know them anyway. She wants to have me be there for her and to always accept her mistakes.

I have other friends who also seem unhappy but not to this extent. And I don't have to be the one to sympathize constantly. On the other hand, when I was down and out and getting a divorce, this friend was wise enough to know it was her turn to listen. And who could understand me better than a friend who has been through so much herself?

The Vulnerability Card

Assuming the Behavior of a Doormat

While her friends may secretly disparage her because of her style of latching on, the doormat knows her worth in spooning out consolation. In Lauren Weisberger's novel *The Devil Wears Prada*, Andy Sachs, the protagonist, acts like a doormat when she tries so hard to please not only her boss, Miranda Priestly, but Emily, Miranda's first assistant (Andy is the second assistant). But Andy is not at all a doormat at heart, and the fashion industry doesn't beckon her enough for her to keep up this front, so she finally breaks free. Another novel that made me think of a friend suppressing herself into a doormat mentality is Susan Minot's *Evening*.

In this story, Ann listens to her friend Lila confess her attraction to Harris, a man other than her fiancé, on the eve of Lila's wedding. All the while, Ann quells her own romantic feelings for Harris and sops up Lila's mixed emotions. The next night, however, Ann and Harris have a brief tryst, which is discovered in the midst of a tragedy. Would Ann have slept with Harris if she'd been a true doormat? It seems unlikely, and the problem, as with Andy Sachs in *The Devil Wears Prada*, is that Ann isn't comfortable with her friend's feelings when she has her own agenda. Both characters' individuality is thinly masked, and of course, when a personal epiphany occurs, the sponging can't be sustained. Evidently, if one is expected to be a doormat by her friends when she isn't really such a friend by personality, she can do so for only so long. Friends find this confusing, and it smacks of betrayal for those who believe someone is a doormat only to discover she is merely pretending.

Consider Dana, 48, an attorney living in D.C., who believes that going back to work after having children caused her to reclaim her former self and discard her doormat-like image.

Since I've become busy professionally, I've lost some second-tier friends. They couldn't stand how tough I'd become after I'd acted so fragile before, when I was at home with my three little children. All those years I acted like a mouse; I listened to these women, these mothers, and I was a good friend. Then I gathered myself together and I changed. I wasn't available to them anymore to listen and say how sorry I was and soothe them.

I think they were surprised that I wasn't quiet anymore. I became loud and bossy, and I didn't ask for favors when it came to carpooling, I demanded it. Those who got insulted couldn't handle it and we stopped being friends. Others hung in, but I know they missed the old me, the one who was pathetic. I wasn't ever really like that; I was biding my time. I always had a plan, and it didn't include these women who were my friends. If they were true friends, they'd stop missing me as some sop and be happy that I'm independent and successful.

Similarly, Nan, 40, who works in advertising and is the mother of two, recounted how for years she listened to her friend Maggie spill all her troubles.

I had this friend and I always had to build her up and listen to her stories. She didn't have a job, her husband left her for someone at his office, her rent was going up too much, her kids were a mess. . . . All this I listened to, and I tried to be supportive. Her upsets made me upset. I had my own problems but rarely time to get a word in. It was okay; it was my job with her. We'd been friends for years. My husband and I included her in so many family events. But one day when I was crazed from work, she leaned on me too much. Right then, I stopped wiping up her messes.

I said, "I can't do this anymore; you give so little back." She was shocked. It hadn't even occurred to her. It was a good time for her to think about what I'd said and to work on herself, but she didn't. She called a few times, hoping to get the old, mild-mannered me back. But that's over. I don't know how it ever even began, but I can't be in a relationship like that anymore. It's like when a woman says, "I need a wife." I need someone to listen to all my misery as opposed to listening to theirs.

A Doormat for the Long Haul

What Way and Greene state in their "Trajectories of Perceived Friendship Quality During Adolescence" is that dependence upon our friends over family begins during our teen years. When this model is applied to adult women, it may or may not be effective. In contrast to Dana and Nan's rejection of the reliant role is Allison, 32, who is a graduate student living in Southern Florida. She is somewhat complacent in the province she established for herself as early as junior high school.

When I was in grade school, I was a kick-ass kind of kid. If I wanted something, I went after it, and if I wanted someone to be my friend, I made it happen. I pushed my mom around and felt like it was my life that mattered. Then I got to junior high and my friends started to have crushes and boyfriends. It wasn't the same, and I lost my hold on things. I gained weight and I did drugs and I began to listen to all their problems without developing my own life or having my own boyfriend. The more I was there for my friends as this supportive dish towel, the more I felt ungrounded. This lasted through college, when I did have a few boyfriends of my own and got my own place. Then I stopped being such a wallflower, but to my friends, who got into a social scene and got engaged, I was still the one left behind. I don't mind not being on the fast track, since the more I listen to their stories, the more I choose a different life. As long as they're still my friends.

If Allison is not able to shake off her assigned role with her friends, at least she has made a decision about it. Danielle, 30, who works in fashion and lives in a Northeastern city, offered insight into how she benefits from her friendship with a doormat, and how it works to her advantage, since she is part leader, part sharer.

I'm the link to all my friends, the one who gets everyone together and who is always at the center of what happens next. I find it easier to be with this one friend from when we were kids because she's always paying attention to what goes on in my life and what matters to me. It might sound really selfish, but as our lives change and some of us are married, or living with a guy and building a career, I can count on this friend—she's always still there for me. Maybe it's lonely for her, and has been for years, but it works for me.

She'll sit on the edge of my bed, eating a bag of Doritos and watching me get dressed for a black-tie party. I can tell her anything, and whenever I'm upset, she'll listen. I'd speak to her ahead of my sisters, my mother, or any other friend, because she doesn't judge. Maybe it's her unhappiness that makes her a better friend. I sometimes wonder what will happen if she does get it together, get a boyfriend or a better job or something. I doubt I'd like it, since she basically shows up for me, within the hour, since we were small. But I'd help her, too, if she needed me to, and I have always invited her to our soirees.

The Plight of the Doormat

In researching this chapter, I noticed that there are few female characters in film, in novels, and on television who can be labeled as authentic doormats. This prototype doesn't lend itself to high drama or to being the star in stories; instead, she might appear as the secondary character in a novel. Not that she isn't curious in her own right, as evidenced in a Jane Austen novel (think of *Northanger Abbey* once the heroine, Catherine Morland, is no longer shielded from a hypocritical society) or an Anita Brookner novel (such as *The Rules of Engagement,* in which Elizabeth, the protagonist, is aware of her own passivity and exclusion). Although these states of heightened awareness are possible, this kind of friend is mostly cautious, is somewhat self-conscious, and can lack personal ambition, like Danielle's friend. Among the classification of friends, the doormat is most unlike the leader.

Interpreting the Doormat

Moral Code. Morality is important to the doormat, although under duress or when influenced by her friends, she is malleable.

Reclusivity. Left to her own devices, the doormat will not initiate social activities; rather, she counts on her friends to invite her.

Shyness. Whether by nature or circumstance, the doormat is not forthcoming emotionally. Nonetheless, when she feels her opinion counts, she'll offer it.

Tendency to Please. Who doesn't welcome a pleaser in our midst? The doormat is keenly aware of this and uses this skill to her advantage.

Once a Doormat, Always a Doormat?

Who doesn't recall how we acted with our friends in high school and how early on we were typecast? While the factors change as we enter new stages of our lives, women often say that the emotions and patterns of these friendships can last a lifetime.

Wearing the Badge: 20-35

There are women who describe feeling "forced" into doormat behavior, positioned as such against their will. Alice, 27, who works in Pennsylvania as a model, recalled how her friend's theft of her boyfriend caused her to lose her place socially as well as to be without her mate.

My close friend Thea stole my boyfriend, but because he was such a big deal, I became the quiet one who had to swallow it all.

I had to stay friends with Thea and I couldn't go to clubs or parties or have the friends I had if I didn't lay low and act like it was okay. The worst part was, this guy isn't even nice; he's just popular. Then Thea started to say how awful he was and she would tell me, as if I didn't know it all too well. I would accept it, and say nothing, not because I didn't have my own thoughts, but because the friend who got him had all the clout. Whatever she says, I say yes, and agree with now. I can't afford to do anything else or I'll be left out. I sometimes wonder if I should move away and start again, or just keep sucking it up till I get a life of my own.

When a woman feels she is subjugated by other women or her social circle, this can be the dark side of a clique or group. In her essay "My Sorority Pledge? I Swore Off Sisterhood," which ran in *The New York Times* on December 2, 2007, Kelly Valen described being ostracized by her sorority sisters. This occurred after she had the unfortunate and demeaning ordeal of drinking too much and being "deflowered" by a fraternity date. The mistreatment of Valen was instigated by one young woman in particular. When this very woman met Valen some twenty years later, it triggered buried memories of dire cruelty. What's so disturbing about the essay, beyond what Valen endured, is how she has been scarred her entire life by an episode in college.

The behavior of her sorority sisters had such an effect upon Valen that she shunned "any kind of group female intimacy," listing baby groups, book clubs, charities, and women's fitness classes among them. When women as leaders of a group of friends, in this case an actual sorority, abuse their power, it is a disservice to female friendship and to women everywhere. Consider Deena, 31, who lives in a Southern city and works part-time in a nursery school. Being banished by her classmates in high school and college for a physical disorder caused Deena to become a consoling figure to her female friends.

I've been so aware of my problems since I was small and kids were really nasty and mean-spirited, especially the girls. What I learned early on, even by sixth grade and definitely in high school, was that if I sympathized with these girls–about homework and sometimes about boys–I could at least be some kind of friend that way. Not that they'd ever include me, but if they needed me, it would work and I could pretend they were real friends. My mother and my sisters weren't very helpful and always shied away from dealing with my social issues. So I had to develop some skills on my own. I was a good student, and that helped; I would let my supposed friends look at my homework and copy it.

I never could face my problem because no one else could. My way of dealing with it was to be available in ways that no one else was. This happened in college too, and only recently have I been able to pull away from this position. I don't want to look for friends with whom I might still be the confidante. I know it's a tool; I just don't want to be used anymore.

Although Deena refined her offerings to her "friends," it is impressive that she was honest with herself about why she was sought out and is now trying to break from her past. Dr. Claire Owen reminds us of the sacrifices we make in order to have friends and keep them: "Some of us have an investment and make a commitment even when the relationship offers little in return. Women don't want to admit to themselves or to others that they've made a poor choice."

While she comes at it from another angle, Brett, 30, who works as a nurse and lives in a small town, recalled how her close-knit circle of friends from high school through their mid-twenties helped one another deal with the abuse in their families.

All that we had was one another. We all had the same needs but were in different places. We all came from psychologically damaged but not broken homes. One friend had a father who was crazy and could be emotionally and physically abusive. Another friend had a father who was an alcoholic. We were bonded and confided in one another, and I was the one who listened the most. I don't know if it's unfortunate or not, but I'm not friendly with this group anymore. I sometimes think we were just lapping up one another's misery, and finally we were looking for ways to break free. One friend had too many issues, and I just politely lost touch; I think that was the beginning of the end. What we did for one another was be some kind of shield, by knowing one another's stuff, and that helped during a really rough period. I suppose we all were doormats, about different things. I didn't have a father, so my problem wasn't about that. I just made the others feel better on that one.

The friends I've made since then also have problems, and I'm the one who tries to make it better, to be not judgmental but sympathetic. I sometimes wonder if I need to find a healthier crowd, maybe some women my age who aren't so battered. But I'll always be the nurse, the one who makes it better.

Sally, 22, who lives in Seattle, where she is currently a part-time student and waitresses, kept her friends' confidences for years. For her, the biggest problem that her friends face is uncertainty about what is ahead in their lives, and their demands on her as a friend plays into this insecurity.

I know most of my girlfriends through work or school, and we're scattered, so it's not a clique. But I'm the goofball story-teller and the one you can bounce ideas off. I'm a good listener, and my friends definitely look to me to confide in. We all have the same problems: Our mothers are crazy, we worry about guys, we worry about girlfriends. I have friends who tell me all their woes, and I can't stand it because they're financially set while I depend on a scholarship plus I work to pay my way through school. So how sorry can I feel for them? But I don't say anything since it's my place to be there to give support when things go wrong. When these friends seem insensitive or spoiled, I stay and give emotional support. I don't feel disappointed as much as they do, so that's why they lean on me. One friend is studying to be a teacher, but she'd rather travel, and I say that's what she should do now, before it's too late, or she'll regret it. So I'm outspoken sometimes, but I also understand everyone's situation. I've always been like this.

When reviewing how being a doormat in terms of female friendship affects younger women, a *New York Times* article by Darcey Steinke, that ran on December 23, 2007, "The Exchange: Kindness for Rudeness," comes to mind. Unlike Kelly Valen, who suffered the consequences of a dishonorable group of sorority sisters, Steinke painted herself as someone who was deliberately spiteful to one of her housemates, named Karen, who might have had the attributes of a doormat; that is, the willingness to assist and bolster a friend.

This took place while Steinke was an American exchange

student in Cork, Ireland, during her junior year in college and believed she was "too good to hang out" with the other young women on the trip; she preferred to be "running around with the college writing crowd." Despite her supposedly appropriate social standing, she admits she was lonely, but remained immutable when Karen attempted to be her friend. Although Steinke continued her icy treatment, Karen aided her when she became sick on Christmas Eve. Maturity plays a part in Steinke's epiphany; as she writes, "It wasn't until years later that I realized what a great gift Karen's kindness had been."

What is notable in this essay is that being a doormat in one's youth has its own psychic rewards. The reliability and companionship factors are worthy, and underscore how female friendships are viewed as "face-to-face" while men's friendships are seen as "side by side," as documented in a study by Paul H. Wright entitled "Men's Friendships, Women's Friendships and the Alleged Inferiority of the Latter." Although there have been hardships, for Deena in particular, the hope of being close to female friends is depicted in the voices of all four interviewees.

Midlife Doormats: 36–50

For women in midlife who have been ravaged by the travesties of life, including divorce, financial setbacks, widowhood, the arduous task of raising children (through adolescence and grappling with the challenges of mothering adult children), any positive interaction with a friend is of great importance. The unfortunate stereotype of women of a certain age is that they are not content. Even the recent prime-time television series about teenagers in New York City attending an Upper East Side private school, *Gossip Girl*, depicts the mothers as unhappy and inaccessible. One can only imagine how women who *do not* have battle wounds but rather are enriched by age and their encounters feel and why they have so little voice. For some veterans, being labeled as the "saint" isn't all bad, and doormat-like tendencies are a plus.

Consider Tabby, 46, who works in the fashion industry and is divorced with three children. Her role with her friends has evolved over time.

My friends come to me because I'm an easy target and I've been through a lot. When someone is dating or getting divorced or getting remarried, I'm the one who never judges but offers a shoulder. I've been around the block, and it doesn't matter to them how I feel, but that I'm a survivor. I used to be the one who was the front runner, the cool friend, but since I got fired and divorced, I'm just the one who can take an earful. Whatever they say, I'm sympathetic and understanding.

My feeling is that I need these friends now more than ever, and so I'm willing to put up with whatever they do. Maybe it's because I'm older, maybe because I was once a big deal in our community and at work and now I'm not. But this is what it is, and I'm satisfied. Are my friends wonderful? No, and it's beside the point. At least I have them around me and it's not just one group through the kids anymore like when they were small, but through work, the gym, neighbors . . . it's all about feeling less isolated and finding people to be with.

Similar to Tabby is Lorie, 48, who works in banking and lives in Florida. Her social life changed when she was divorced several years ago; her new life places her in a less visible light.

Before I had to work full-time I was in a clique and I was the "it" wife. This was a group of people who did the same things and were together with our husbands, too, as couples. The women all loved the same sports and traveled together. We didn't exactly treat one another as equals, and I made sure of that. But we pretended to be equal, and I was happy to be there in my position. Since my husband and I split up, my life has changed dramatically, and I've lost some friends and made new ones. I now am more willing to take what I can get, and I'm a realist. I know that in this city, no one treats a divorcée very well. I want to still have a life, so I hang on to my old friends, and for them, I'm the one who cleans the floor. It's hard to take since I wasn't like that before.

With my new friends, I decided to be the one who pleases everyone and is really adaptable. I figured it would be better this way and decided to not be so loud now. I don't have the money anymore, and I've taken on two jobs to make ends meet. At work, I am the convenient one to go to with a problem. Some of these women are as miserable as I am, so that's okay. Sometimes I don't even pay attention anymore to their problems; I just act like I care.

What is resonant for both young women and women in midlife who fit the definition of a doormat is the deliberate choice to be situated in this way. While some women come by this role naturally, and have a shyer and more reserved style, there are others who emerge in this mode after a major life change. For those on the receiving end, the doormat can be reassuring and attentive, but that isn't always enough to make a friendship work. For instance, the trophy friend is looking for someone who will be devoted, exclusively hers, and we know the doormat is capable of this. However, the trophy friend also becomes impatient when the doormat is too eager to please, because securing the doormat's devotion isn't much of a hurdle. After a while, this becomes apparent in the friendship and the attachment feels flawed.

An example of this is Michele, a self-described trophy friend (more on this in Chapter 7), who finds that the excitement of being with a friend can dilute other parts of one's life. Michele, 46, is a married mother of two, lives in a rural area, where she works in a physician's office. Michele confessed that her friend Andrea, who falls into the doormat category, is often irritating.

It always happens the same way. At first, it's all great and Andrea and I are raring to go. We plan day trips into the city, and we plan our holidays around each other's families. We talk on the phone and exchange e-mail to make plans, and I'm sure it's going to be perfect. When we get together, finally, since we hardly have time with our work schedules to do it unless it's planned, we're so happy. We talk and gossip, we trade sob stories about our husbands. Then, after a few hours or a few days of this, it sort of falls apart. Whatever I tell Andrea, she agrees with, and she doesn't seem to have a thought in her head that's her own. I get tired of her echoing me—if I'm voting Republican, so is she; if I'm voting Democrat, so is she. If I like a restaurant, so does she, and it's ... annoying after a while.

Then I remember how I am so close to my other women friends and how they feel more like equals. But no one is easier on me than Andrea. In fact, she doesn't have an idea in her head. I'm safer with her than with anyone else among my friends, so what if she's nondescript and desperate. Maybe she isn't the most interesting person and maybe she's boring, but there are days when I'm grateful she's not the hard work that some friends demand.

Michele's interaction with Andrea indicates that women are able to connect with each other without a common bond, based instead on a common need. Andrea is taxing to Michele after some time together, but this association works for both women. It actually provides relief for Michele, since being a trophy friend is undeniably tiring, and she's aware of this.

Seasoned Absorbers: 51–70

Mature women have been at the game of female camaraderie for decades, and there isn't much that surprises them. A majority of women report that at this stage in their lives, a doormat is an indispensable friend to have, the keeper of a friend's secrets and faithful to a fault. Most women of this age who fill the shoes of the doormat have had a few eye-openers along the way and have settled into the role, but there are those doormats who continue to feel compromised with their friends.

An example of the latter is Ella, 54, who is remarried with grown children. She clings to her ruthless group of friends at work, though the endless incidents unnerve her.

I hang on to the women at work when they aren't really my friends because I can't be without them. I kiss up and am always nicest to the one in charge since she's been there forever and knows the ropes. She's someone you wouldn't upset and I'm very careful about it. I am not only nice to her but I also worry because she can turn on people; I've seen it go on. I tell myself I'd escape this if it wasn't about work, but I'm not sure. Ultimately, it's like I'm still in high school—not even college, where I could find other outlets. Work is hardest. It's my livelihood, and I'm not going to jeopardize anything, so this woman is my friend, absolutely.

What I do is act as if I care about her life. I nod when she complains about her kids, her dog, her share of the profits, her husband—all of it. I know it's a cutthroat business and I know that my friends outside the office aren't as tough. There I can be myself, but here I'm the dishrag and it's been this way for years. I'm wiser, but I play the same game at the office as I did decades ago.

While Ella believes this is the right tack to take regarding work friends, Julie, 56, a single mother with one child who lives in Rhode Island, represents someone with a personal history of the ins and outs of female friendships.

I've been at this for years. I've shied away from the friends who are too demanding, too messed up, but I've stayed with the ones who appreciate me. I remember how nasty my mother was to her friends, to her sister, and to us. She was so angry and bitter. She demanded so much of her friends. That's when I knew I wanted my friendships to work out. I became the martyr for my friends unless they dragged me down too much. That I learned way back in college. And then years later I had a friend who said bad things about my son when he was young. Though I didn't want to make waves, I had to say something. I was level-headed and she wasn't, and I think she resented me. But I tried not to be emotional; I held it together.

I look back on how I've managed with some wrong friends and how I also was able to leave when someone was jumping down my throat. Today I'm the same kind of friend, but I have a bit of wisdom. My friends are very important to me, and if my misgivings are small, I don't make a fuss. I don't want to be alone.

Loneliness and the Doormat

Julie raises the issue of loneliness, which is applicable to women of all ages and is threaded throughout this book. Doormats will confess that their technique is a method of staving off this feeling. Consider Martha, 70, who is twice widowed, without children, and lives in a retirement community. She explains how being a doormat is expedient.

I moved here five years ago and then my husband died. The women were kind of standoffish and no one wanted to be my friend when there were so many single women already. I made a decision that if I was someone who would go out, take chances, drive at night, I would have a few friends. So I went to the gym, I played golf, and I became the chauffeur for evening events in order to be a commodity, and still it wasn't easy. As soon as I made it clear that I wasn't competing for the handful of men around here, that I was just looking for some women friends, things worked out better. At night it's quiet and sometimes it's lonely, but during the day I'm busy with my new friends. Right now I want to be with the women more than I want to find another guy, so I'm okay with taking a backseat on this. I hear everyone's story and I'm supportive; I'm ready to do what it takes.

Reciprocity and the Doormat: Who Pays Her Back?

Barbara Kellerman's book *Followership: How Followers Are Creating Change and Changing Leaders* asserts that followers are of the same magnitude as leaders. According to her book, followers and leaders are inseparable. Although doormats aren't pure followers, they do have attributes of followers; consequently, the leader and the doormat dance a duet. A doormat's raison d'être is compounded by a culture that rewards less-than-aggressive goal-oriented actions for women. No wonder a doormat finds a place among other types of female friends and feels welcome.

The primary question becomes whether any of these friends show gratitude for the doormat, who isn't aggressive, but compliant. As Deena, whom we met earlier, remarked, the recognition isn't easy to come by.

I got lots of phone calls from the girls in my class the night before a paper was due or a test was going to be given. Not that anyone ever thanked me for what I did or acknowledged it. I did it because I had to; I had no other way.

The Expedience Factor

Among women, the friend who soaks up a misdemeanor and is able to look the other way might be at an advantage. This is especially true when dependence on friendship looms large. While some could judge a woman who does this as lacking self-respect, there are those interviewees who recognize the bargain they have made, and see a reward for their behavior. Although half of the interviewees for this chapter felt coerced into doormat mode, the 25 percent who are natural-born doormats are comfortable with their role and their concessions. Ten percent of doormats were able to turn over a new leaf after many years, and became more assertive. Fifteen percent felt that having a friend who is a doormat benefits them, if not necessarily the doormat herself.

In some scenarios, the nuances of doormat status are tied into a woman's maturity; in others, they are about long-standing friendships. Dr. Ronnie Burak remarks, "There's a self-confidence in getting older, and women tend to treat friends better at that stage. Later in life, women value friends more. Women can feel very alone in the world and haven't a clue of this when they're young." Antonia, 39, who works in a pet store in a small town, has realistic expectations of her friend who is a doormat.

Who else would put up with all of my moods and baggage but my one friend who has been so steady (and sort of boring) since high school? She is an angel when it comes to my stuff, and I ask a lot. She doesn't seem to care; she's always been like this. I think she's happy being the one who can be supportive—she's there to do the cleanup.

The Intricacies of Befriending a Doormat

Do you feel smothered by your friendship with the doormat?

Perhaps it is time to distance yourself and make this known to her. Or perhaps your circumstances are now different and what you once appreciated feels stifling.

Do you feel the boundaries are blurred, that she doesn't have original thoughts but emulates your ideas?

If your doormat feels like a shadow, healthy boundaries need to be established. If this doesn't bother you and you know it's how she is, then overlook it.

Is your doormat steadfast in a way that trumps the drain game of being with her sometimes?

When the doormat is a valued friend, her good intentions win you over, and this creates a lasting friendship. There are women who welcome their doormat because she is steady in her style and her devotion.

The Profit for the Doormat

Do you find yourself reserved and empathetic by nature?

If so, then being a doormat works for you and the benefits outweigh any negativity. If you are a doormat in order to ingratiate yourself with a few women, then it isn't going to last and will feel unnatural eventually.

Is it a relief that there is little drama surrounding your friendships?

Doormats tend to accommodate a friend to avoid confrontation or upsets. This comes in handy when you seek a quiet friendship that has few bumps and disturbances.

Does being on the A-list mean little to you, or do you feel denied?

If you feel entitled to a better life and unrewarded for your efforts, you should consider defining yourself differently. If you are happy to take a backseat, then your role in the scheme of female friendships is working for you. As the recipient of your gestures, it's best to have a friend who is settled in her style and content.

THREE

The Sacrificer: Blind Spots

✗ Does this friend make herself available when no one
   else would?
✗ Is she unable to face it when a friend is conten-
   tious?
✗ Does she disregard a friend's competitive nature
   because she wants the friendship desperately?
✗ Is she hell-bent on offering unconditional support?
✗ Despite her support, could this friend be jealous of
   you?

**If your friend fits any of the descriptions above, you are dealing
with a sacrificer.**

"If my husband or children need me, I cancel any plans with my
closest girlfriend. But if the friend persists, I'll see her and go out
of my way for her too," explained Ruthie, 34, who is a social worker
with three children, living in the Pacific Northwest. "Then I'm on

triple overload, but I know I've been a good friend and I will do what it takes. Basically she tells me her sob story and I offer to do things that I can't really add to my responsibilities. Like have her dog come to our house, since my dog hates her dog. On top of it, I have a demanding mother and a sister who isn't married. They call all the time, as if I don't work and have three kids under six and a husband. My mother will say to me, 'If you don't mind . . . ,' and so I say, 'Of course not.'

"Sometimes my best friend reminds me of my mother; there's always a glitch, and I'm the person to call. I find my children and my husband to be easier to deal with than my friend. But we've been friends for so long, and we were single together. I think I owe it to her to go out of my way. Meanwhile, she's saying things to me like that I married down and that she wouldn't have settled. I say nothing; I know it's not true and she's just unhappy. I do the best I can for her, or for how I feel about myself when I do it."

Although the **sacrificer** at first appears to be similar to the doormat, and these types of friends might cross over, her position in the realm of female friendship carries another kind of weight altogether. The sacrificer is the one who takes the leap for her friends, and in tough times, we lean on this person, who will answer her phone in the dead of night to console you. The sacrificer's search for closeness is often what motivates her, and she is confident that she can handle a friend's expectations. When a sacrificer discovers that her friends are less dedicated than she, she can be very disappointed. There are also those sacrificers who have ulterior motives and might not remain in a friendship in which, despite their sacrifices, the outcome is less than gratifying.

In a perfect world, sacrificers and those for whom they

have sacrificed would be content. In fact, the demands of a fast-paced, multilayered society contribute to the fraying of friendships for the most hopeful of sacrificers. The composite interview below indicates how far the sacrificer will go for a friend. Both the sacrificer herself and anyone who is close to her know that the sacrificer's fortune is based on the friend's response to her earnestness. When this falls apart, the sacrificer feels like she's lost out.

The Dismantled Team

For years you and your closest friend have been a team. When you first started out, working in the same city, you traveled to work together and met at the health club most evenings. You both climbed the corporate ladder and shared your travails with men, and you nursed her through several miserable love affairs. No matter what went on in your life, you had this best friend, and you put her first. There were Christmas dinners that you shared, and a few New Year's Eves as well. What was implicit was how faithful you were to her in terms of time and availability.

Her relocation to another city was a blow; you promised to visit every holiday, to continue to travel together on vacations, and to not lose any of the closeness. To ease her transition, you contacted an old friend from college who lives in her new city and insisted that she reach out to your friend. After a few months, your friend's numerous e-mails and phone calls fell off. You purchased your ticket to visit for her birthday anyway, as planned. The price was exorbitant, but you didn't want to be there any time but her actual birthday. Once you arrived, you were astonished to learn that your closest friend had become engaged. As out of the loop as you had become, quite dispensable, you make the decision to hang on, however you can, to the friendship. You offer to host a celebration lunch (despite your lack of finances) back home for her. After all, what are friends for?

Visual Impairments

Losing sight of our own rules in a friendship is a frequent issue for the sacrificer. On occasion, the sacrificer can cause the end of a friendship by not confronting a situation. This transpired when Gina, 40, who lives in Rhode Island, where she works at a radio station, lost touch with a dear friend.

I had a girlfriend and we were really close. We would walk our dogs together every night and trade confidences. She just dropped me one day and I couldn't understand why. Years later when I saw her she told me my boyfriend at that time had come on to her. She was so uncomfortable that I lost her as a friend. I wonder what I would have done had I known. What bothers me is that she never gave me a chance. We'd done so much together, and in truth, she was the giving friend—the one who reached out to me. She asked very little of me and made all these plans, gave all this energy to us.

I would have preferred to have talked about the matter with her and to have known everything. Her final way of giving, I suppose, was to not make that happen, to not make me have to choose or feel torn about anything. But I'm the type who wants information and can handle confrontation—I doubt she could.

While the upside of female friendship is feeling understood by and known to each other, a failed friendship such as Gina's is proof of how little we comprehend sometimes. Consider Robin, 50, who lives in Oregon and works in publicity. She is married with one daughter.

I have this one friend who always used to blow me off for a guy, a movie, anything that came up. I was really pissed but I put up with it for years. I remember before I got married, nine years ago, I could tell her anything. But not anymore. So I never plan anything with much enthusiasm because I know it doesn't pan out with her at the end. On my side, I've driven hours to see her, worked on my schedule to make it gel with hers, included her after I had a child and a husband and she didn't. I feel like we've been a romantic couple for years and I'm the more interested partner. I'm unhappy with the result, and I feel that I've put too much into this to be in this position.

Dr. Donald Cohen, a psychologist, points out that the level of involvement of women in female friendships can be high on the list of emotional minefields. "When something goes awry with a close female friend, it's emotionally charged. Only breaking up a family due to divorce is more devastating. With female friends, it's hard to leave, and dicey to stop the patterns." The women I interviewed echo this observation; women suffer a void when one friend expects more than another.

Maria Malihiosi-Loizos and Lynn Anderson investigate the distinction between accessible friendship and inclusive friendship. The "accessible friend" is the one we can call but do not include in social events; meanwhile, the "inclusive friend" is the one we invite but might not call and lean on. Women tell me that they feel disenfranchised without the latter. Malihiosi-Loizos and Anderson point out that the lack of reciprocity is an issue. "If mutuality or reciprocity does occur," they write, "the new acquaintance could become an important and possibly intimate friend." If not, the new person will be merely an "acquaintance," and this creates loneliness, which looms large for women. But a sacrificer will go the distance to avoid the letdown and to earn the reward. No wonder it is so devastating when it doesn't work out for this kind of friend.

What could feel more counterproductive to the sacrificer than to feel that she has failed at her mission? In her quest to get it right, she might excuse less-than-exemplary behavior in her friends.

Few of us truly know ourselves, let alone those we invite in and with whom we trade confidences. The same sentimental trap that women fall into when they fall in love with a man, being smitten by the illusion rather than the reality, can also affect their relationships with women friends. We can apply the first two thirds of psychologist and author Robert J. Sternberg's theory of heterosexual love, intimacy and commitment, to this equation; the third ingredient, passion, becomes the differential between romantic love and female friendship. In this way, intimacy and commitment are enough to blindside female friends, and women don't always "see" the friend for who she really is. In walks the sacrificer, who is ready to throw herself at the friendship despite the blind spots. Having a clear vision of a friend and who she truly is reveals itself in assorted ways.

For instance, Jill, 55, who works as a high school principal and lives in North Carolina, where she raised three sons, recognizes the friends who will go out of their way for her.

I would do whatever a close friend needs and I'd be there for her in a flash. I learned this from my father, who taught me how to be giving. My mother less so, but my father was soft and gentle and knew what friendship was about. For me it's about give-and-take. I have a friend who complains a lot, but underneath I know she'd do as much for me as I would do for her. She's one of my closest friends because of that and I look the other way when she whines. I've had some friends who seem sincere but aren't and I've gone out of my way for some friends who haven't returned the favor. So I think I know the difference. Years ago I was naive and my husband's business required that I befriend some of the wives of his clients. But they weren't friends—they only seemed that way. This friend who is always feeling lousy or for whom something is always wrong, she's the real thing.

Jill has consciously chosen friends who are sacrificers like herself. If she recognizes a friend as being disloyal, she moves on, representing a sacrificer who has perameters.

Though I know I'm a good and loyal friend and I'd sacrifice for a friend, I have high hopes, and I'm an old-timer. I am so careful about whom I let in and what people want from me. I've learned this through some rough times when I thought someone wanted me for me but she wanted me for what I could do for her. These friends were phonies, and I was so hurt at first—I wanted my time back or my good deed back. Now I seem to know the difference right off the bat and I stay clear. I only go with loyal friends, and I'm very loyal and giving in return.

Chain of Command

There are some arresting twists to sacrificers in terms of the hierarchy of female friendship, and the issue of mutual commitment hovers beneath the surface. Jill, who is secure in the reciprocity of her friendships, doesn't balk at leaving a friend who isn't up to par. Consider Laurie, 35, who works for a corporation in a Northeastern city and claims that she would sacrifice for a certain friend and not for others.

I favor this friend, not because she's so nice, because she isn't. And not because what she does is so great, because it's only about how it works best for her. Still, I'd do anything for this friend, and in her own screwy way, she does the same for me—just not at my level. We have one or two other friends and they definitely deserve better from us, but we don't come through for them. Instead, it's her and me, and we keep pouring it on for each other. Sometimes the other friends make noise about it and see us as really exclusive and unfair to the rest of the crowd. We talk about them and we act better than they are sometimes. It won't change; it's how we are.

Heather, 24, who lives in Northern California, where she works at a hospital, has sacrificed within a group of friends, as has Laurie. Her style is to be acrobatic, rearranging her schedule for any of the three women in her crowd.

Four of us all worked together and there was a lot of immature behavior that went on over plans that were changed or canceled. I usually was the one to bend over backward, to change my work schedule to be there. I'd say, Sure, okay, and then postpone a night with my boyfriend or my mom for these friends, only to be blown off or to find out that the plan had changed again. So when things got inconvenient for me, I'd go crazy making it all work. I'd hang out with them when it wasn't what I should have been doing, and I'd do things at work to make it easier for them.

When it doesn't feel good, it still takes me a long time to let it go, and that's what finally happened. It all became such a drag, and I knew I had to stop trying and giving up myself and my life for these friends. Breaking something off when you're all at the same place every day takes real guts, but I did it. And I've made some new friends; not work friends. It's healthier, but already I can see I'm the one who would do more for these friends than they'd do for me.

We see how Heather fits the sacrificer mold, and while she's courageous enough to change, she already fears falling into the same pattern with her newfound friends. It makes us question not only the ramifications of breaking our traditional behavior when the opportunity arises, but why the purity of a sacrificer such as Heather becomes a liability rather than an asset.

Not that we aren't drawn to a virtuous friend who gives her time and energy to friendship, as evidenced in the Disney romantic comedy *Enchanted*. Giselle, played by Amy Adams, is an innocent friend/mother hen to all the animals in the forest in her happy world of animation. She teaches them all that she knows, and they in turn protect her. Once Giselle is banished to the gritty real world of New York City by the evil Queen Narissa, played by Susan Sarandon, her innocence and sacrificing tendencies are put to the test. It is Giselle's everlasting optimism that makes her so endearing; she is a genuine sacrificer from start to finish. She embraces Patrick Dempsey's character, Robert Philip's, young daughter, Morgan, played by Rachel Covey, with great enthusiasm. As Seth Shulman, a psychotherapist whose practice includes women's issues, notes, the sacrificer has strong maternal instincts. "Most sacrificers work harder at relationships and are twice as clever at sacrificing for the friend and working it into their schedule, if necessary."

Chameleons: Social-Climbing Sacrificers

At least Queen Narissa was obvious in her desire to destroy Giselle, and the only posturing she did that might have made her appear giving was when she twice offered Giselle the poisonous apple. On a less dire level are those sacrificers who realize that it might be in their nature to be giving, but that it's best when one sacrifices for a reward. In this way, altruism is woven with opportunity and sacrifice, and the motivation of a sacrificer is applied as a means to an end. Consider Nadine, 50, who lives in Santa Fe, where she runs a family business.

I learned years ago that as long as I'm gong the distance for a friend, it might as well be worth my while. I apply this to work since I'm a workaholic and so many of my friends are through business; the others belong to my social circle. If a friend can do something for me on either count, great, but mostly I do for them. I carpooled way out of my way for my younger son because I knew the other child's mother was important socially. I've had events at my home, fund-raisers, because it helps with work. So I'm giving, but for a return on my investment. When I was in high school, I was friendly with the popular crowd, and I'd do the same thing for one of those girls then. I never complained, and I was constant; I sympathized with their misery and offered to help out. I think it works well.

Nadine's view of her calculated sacrificing reminds me, in a less dramatic way, of Pat Conroy's novel *The Prince of Tides*. The tale of the Wingo family of Colleton, South Carolina, is told through Tom's memories of this unhappy, shrimp-fishing, impoverished family. One of the pivotal events in his chronicle is his mother's devotion to her terminally ill friend. Lila Wingo devotes enough time to nursing this wealthy woman at her home, waiting on her on a continual basis, that she gets to know the husband. Once he is widowed, she marries him, therefore benefiting from her sacrifice. While this character's behavior and the result appear quite deliberate, another form of a social-climbing sacrificer is characterized by Rory, who has come to realize that the purest of intentions often go unappreciated. Her trajectory is the result of this awareness.

Rory, 41, who works in marketing and lives in Michigan, has decided to put her sacrifices to good use.

Why should I always give up my Sunday for my friend who insists that we meet in her neighborhood? Why do I always have to help my other best friend, who is never without a crisis? One weekend I'm moving her to her new place after a long day of work, and the next I'm painting her place or taking her cat to the vet or listening to her sob story of the week. I'm steady, always there, the rock. I bend over backward with my friends, and it's my own fault. These are my closest friends—we've been friends forever, and I never realized until recently that they aren't very appreciative, neither of them. Then my mother pointed out that I'm a middle child, so I aim to please. I'm the one who does everything for everyone else.

I decided to be like these friends, who just ask and ask. I didn't stop giving, I just stopped turning into whatever they needed: plumber, mover, painter. I started to expect something back, and I made it clear to them. I told one of the friends that she could watch my cat as easily as I could watch hers. I asked her to help paint my house before I moved in. It isn't that my needs were so different, but I never asked before. It took years for me to even the scales, to turn into someone who could ask of them, too.

Equal Playing Fields: Affinity Versus Necessity

According to a study conducted by Karen Rook, "Reciprocity of Social Exchange and Social Satisfaction Among Older Women," reciprocity—lessening loneliness by establishing a relationship of give-and-take between friends—varies as a means of social exchange. The standard of reciprocity applies to friendships between the sacrificer and others, and this issue seems applicable to women throughout their lives. This becomes apparent in the case of Nadine's attitude toward her friends, Rory's constantly demanding friend, and, in Conroy's novel, Lila Wingo's plan to nurse her ill friend.

Doormat + Sacrificer = A Wearisome Friendship

Although there are positive doormats (more on this in Chapter 9, "The Sharer") and positive sacrificers, when the two categories overlap, a sense of unease may ensue for the friend on the receiving end. The way that Allison, 38, who works in the arts and lives in Omaha, portrays her close friend Claudia, a doormat/sacrificer, her needs are thinly veiled cries for help.

My friend Claudia and I were roommates in college years ago. I knew from the day I met her that her life was troubled and that she was also special. She could hear your pain and come up with some good advice, and she was more available than any other friend, but it was always about her. I thought she was so understanding all those years ago when we complained about course loads and boys and other friends, but somehow when we got around to her, it was exhausting. We once drove to another school for the weekend. She said that she was doing me a favor by sharing the driving and our confidences, but I felt wrung out by the end and guilty for feeling that way.

Now that we're adult women with kids and ex-husbands, she still drains me, and the implication is that she's doing me the favor. She manages to present herself as some selfless being, patient, trusting, and as someone who has gone out of her way for me. It isn't the case at all. I feel that I'm working hard to please her and working around her schedule. She's really good at being the martyr. I can't get her to stop being this way, and we have too much history to ever not be friends.

If Allison is exhausted by her doormat/sacrificer, she remains committed to the relationship nonetheless. Maura, 43, who works as a consultant and lives in Idaho, feels that her best friend is someone who rarely asks about her these days but who has been there for her in the past.

I have this one friend who is really self-involved. We've been friends for so long, through highs and lows, that I can say we'll always be friends. She doesn't have as many friends as I do, and at the moment she's not dating, while I live with someone. That's why when I'm sick of listening to her problems and tired of running to pick up one of her kids, I remind myself that we're friends for the long haul. Meanwhile, everyday phone calls in which she doesn't ask a word about me or my kids or my financial worries but goes on about hers for hours are annoying.

On the other hand, during my divorce, I leaned on her, and I had no one else. She had to watch my kids and hers when I worked late hours. My crisis is past and hers might never be, it seems, but I remind myself of those two years when I drained her. Now my luck has changed and she needs to drain me.

Who Would You Sacrifice For?

In the feature film *The Big Chill*, Glenn Close plays Sarah Cooper, the wife of Kevin Kline's Harold Cooper. When Meg Jones, played by Mary Kay Place, Sarah's best friend from college, confides that she hasn't found the right guy and is frantic that her biological clock is running out, Sarah offers up her husband for a night. The far-reaching consequences of this generous gesture are obvious. Trust is at a premium, and in terms of being a doormat/sacrificer, Close's character, Sarah, is at the pinnacle. In real life, such a gesture could be too loaded to occur; the risks outweigh the good deed. For example, Jenny, 39, who divorced her husband and confessed to her best friend, a doormat/sacrificer, all of her discontent in the marriage, got a low blow: She soon learned that her ex-husband is now dating this woman. Jenny, who works in pharmaceuticals and lives in New Hampshire, believes that she unloaded too much information.

I have begun to doubt myself ever since my best friend and my husband took up together. I made her listen to me during my divorce, and she had to take in all these stories. I was angry at him, and I told her so. Maybe I made him look bad; I don't know. But she sure was my crutch; she was at my side day and night. She drove to see me when I was too down to drive to her part of town. She brought pizza and movies to watch. She commiserated with me and told me war stories about her own divorce years before. She broke dates with guys to babysit me through this terrible time. She said bad things about my ex because I wanted her to, and then she stopped. I'm not sure how they got together, but they did—maybe through some sporting event for our older boys. I didn't like to go, so this friend would be there for both of us. I know my ex would go—he always did—and maybe that's what happened.

Once their secret got out in this little town, she tried to stay friends with me, but I let it go. I felt she'd really betrayed me, and I don't speak to her. I don't know when she stopped being my rock during my divorce and began to betray me. I lost a friend I really needed, and I think she needed me—until she wanted my ex-husband more than our friendship.

The Tipping Point: True and Untrue Sacrificers

It is a curveball for those whose sacrificer has betrayed them. Since the sacrificer, whether she crosses over with the doormat or not, appears to be an unlikely candidate for this kind of behavior (although she can be a social climber), the negative stories shared by the interviewees in this category have a rawness to them. In any close relationship, trust is a major factor. Yet, as we've heard in the interviewees' voices, even a sacrificer might be induced to put her wishes above those of her friends and, in this way, cause a breach. As we will see in future chapters, trust isn't at the heart of the matter for the user or for the trophy friend, but in this category, it is applicable.

Therefore, the sacrificer with motives of her own delivers a double whammy—the giving friend is deceitful. And because the sacrificer is well aware of how she is perceived and who she is supposed to be, she begins to doubt her mission. Consider Janice, 57, who sells real estate in Maryland and is divorced with grown children. She retired as the odd girl out in a long-standing friendship.

There was this uneven treatment of me that finally took me over the top with my two best friends. We grew up like sisters, and whoever needed help got it. I was the one who did the most helping, and after a while, I began to feel like a middle child and that I was being squeezed out of the good parts. This went on for years, through college, our weddings, our divorces, one of us getting remarried . . . and as the years went on, I was the one helping, and no one was helping back.

Everyone talked like we were the same, the same to one another, with the same amount of give-and-take. A few years ago, I found out that they'd rented a little cottage together for a month in the summer and didn't include me, just asked me for the weekend. That's when I knew the trust wasn't there anymore, and they weren't really my close friends. I wouldn't have done this to them, and it was time to face it. It made me face a few things too, like that for Christmas, they bought each other great gifts and I got the pashmina from the street. It was time to be smart about it.

Sacrificers as Enablers

Part of Altman and Taylor's theory, put forth in their book, *Social Penetration: The Development of Interpersonal Relationships,* is that when a relationship begins, there is an evaluation of payment and expense. When it becomes too "expensive," the relationship ceases to exist. This concept can be applied to close female friendships in which one woman is defined as the sacrificer. And as in a romantic relationship that is deficient, it plays out with a beginning, a middle, and an end. Ironically, as we'll recognize in the various chapters, when it comes to close female friendships, more women stay the course than not. A sacrificer who finds a friendship trying and disappointing may complain and suffer but remain with the friend, continuing in her role as the giving one.

As Lauralee, 24, who works as a bartender in New England, explained it, her commitment supersedes her friendship with someone who takes advantage.

I've had this close friend, a family friend, since I was two. After high school, I realized it wasn't a friendship but a habit. I couldn't count on her, but she could count on me when she needed me. She called and I was there, of course. This went on since junior high. Meanwhile, she wasn't there for me and I was always disappointed. Once in a while she'd pretend she was there, like she'd taken some lessons from me, but she didn't want to be like that, to be doing all that I needed. When we were younger we bonded over extra school-work, lying to our moms about where we'd been, cutting class, smoking pot. Later on it was about boys mostly and life, just trying to grow up. Again, I'd do whatever she wanted, and she'd somehow not have to do much for me.

It goes on now, today, when I've moved away from home and she's still there. It's the same story, and I say and do the same thing, long distance. I'd say that she's the lucky one. There's not much upside in saying something to her, so I do what I do, for her and for myself.

If it is difficult for Lauralee to turn her back on her child-hood friend although there's not much return on her sacri-fices, Nora, 29, who works as an office manager in New Jersey, admitted that it was easier for her to cancel her wedding than to end an unproductive best friendship.

Quite honestly, this friendship issue never goes away. Guys come and go, and I give those guys my all. Or so I think until I re-member what I've done for one or two friends. One I let go; I had to, it was so destructive. And everyone knew us as close friends, so it was visible, just like my broken engagement. But the other friend, the one I'd die for, I am around for, no matter what. I will do any-thing she asks; I think it got in the way of my engagement, that my fiancé resented her. She's impossible, and sometimes I think she's crazy, but I'm also such a pathetic one, doing whatever she needs, and she is needy. Maybe I'm needy, too, and I need her. Whatever it is, we're a couple, sort of; it's not like a guy who finally does too much damage and you cut out.

Endgame for the Sacrificer

Nora's take on her role as the sacrificer and her object of sacrifice sums up the level of dedication and emotional connection that goes on. Despite the struggles, the yield for the sacrificer and for those for whom she sacrifices is high. The notion that the friend-ship could improve motivates the sacrificer, and she makes the decision to stay in 50 percent of the cases in this chapter. Thirty percent of the sacrificers felt it was time to distance themselves from those for whom they sacrificed, and the other 20 percent were dismissed by their friends, despite their sacrifices.

To Sacrifice or Not to Sacrifice

Does your sacrificer, who puts her heart and soul into the relationship, expect an exchange of information?
A sacrificer who feels she is getting shortchanged is often hurt and unhappy with her friend/s. In these instances, the friend could be more sympathetic to how the sacrificer feels.

Why is it that when the writing is on the wall that she's no longer needed, she still doesn't get it?
Some sacrificers are too tenacious for their own good and need to listen up. For others, they will always be this way and move on to someone who needs them if they sense that their friends are no longer appreciative.

Why does the sacrificer get "used" by her friends?
Many times she is too immersed in her plan to realize the situation (more on this in Chapter 5, "The User"). Sacrificers

are often underrated. This is unfortunate, and her friends
might consider what she brings to the table.

What if you are with a sacrificer who is also a user?

Do not underestimate that sacrificers who are users exist. This
blend can confuse the issue for the innocent friend, and it isn't
always a satisfying result. For others, full awareness on the part
of both the sacrificer/user and her friend is enough to make it
work.

FOUR

The Misery Lover: Down and Out

✗ Does this friend rely on unhappiness to hold the friendship together?

✗ Do you trust and believe in the energy and time she gives to you?

✗ Does she deny that this is a friendship of convenience?

✗ Does she offer her inner secrets, hoping to know yours?

✗ Is this a friend who cares about mutual benefits?

If your friend is someone who sees life this way, she is a misery lover.

"Years ago, this friendship was better, especially when we first became close; we had boyfriends, who were friends, so it was a constant double date," said Hailey, 36, who lives in the Southeast and works in marketing. "Then we had job hunts during our senior year of college and we decided to rent a house-share on weekends in the summer. We'd both just broken up with our college boy-friends the same month. That was when we told each other every-thing—I knew I could count on her. I was in worse shape, falling apart over my boyfriend, and she was like a tower of strength. The thing was, though, that our lives were so similar.

"But after that, we went our separate ways and I got married and pregnant while she lived with the same guy for years. I didn't like him and I doubt that he liked me, so that made things harder for us. Plus I kept having children and she was still not married. I tried to include her in family parties, kids' birthday parties, but this might have made it worse. Now when I see her, I think she's jealous or angry or something because my life is busy with kids, my hus-band, and my job. She never married and isn't happy with work, or so she says. I doubt she wants to hear about me anymore."

Enough women describe their **misery lover** as a friend who cares more about your bad news than your good news. These friends rally when a crisis hits and are even able to make a small incident into a bigger problem, at times. Although we find this friend consoling when the chips are down—if you've gained weight or lost your job, had a fight with your sister or mother, begun divorce proceedings, or are suffering along with an unhappy child—when the situation improves, she distances herself. The misery lover can cross over with the mirroring friend, the doormat, the sacrificer, and the authen-tic friend (until she leaves you), but her MO is definitely based on the "misery loves company" precept.

There are those friendships with a misery lover where the friends are so close, as Hailey described, that they finish each other's sentences. However, once they've gone their separate ways, though these two friends have managed to remain friendly, there is tension in the relationship today. In my research for my book *Tripping the Prom Queen: The Truth About Women and Rivalry*, I labeled women's expecting that their friends will reflect their reality and merge because their journeys are so similar the "twinning syndrome."

Yet even the best of friends tend to have differences in personal style, and to think that we are all in it in the same way can get us into trouble and, unfortunately, keep us less open to friends who are not like us. Much of friendship among women is environmental and age related, but preconceived notions of each other also factor into the relationship. Women who have found someone initially off-putting and "not their style" can be pleasantly surprised, and such prejudices or early impressions can be overcome. Therefore, it's unfortunate for friends who cling together because of what they have in common when one diverges from this path, especially when she improves her situation and the other feels she has been forsaken. Consider the composite below of several misery lovers and their take once the friend is in a better place.

Operating Instructions

For years you and your friend have traded confidences. When she was married ten years ago and said that money was a huge problem for her and her husband, you listened. When she said that it ruined their honeymoon, you hung on every detail and called him a cad. Later, when her mother-in-law became another source of friction in her marriage, you enjoyed all the stories and agreed that her mother-in-law was a controlling, horrible woman—the source of all her husband's bad attitudes. This friend would call you at all hours about her husband's spending habits. When he put her on a budget since she wasn't working and then played three rounds of golf one weekend, you suggested she leave him. She was listening to your advice, and crying about loving him but feeling so frustrated, when she landed an impressive job. Suddenly she didn't care as much that he wanted to be in charge of the money.

This was a cog in the works for sure, not only because you have had such ups and downs with your career, and because your boyfriend just moved out. Plus, your friend decided to work with her husband on their "issues." Suddenly your advice seemed out of date and stale to your more upbeat friend. In fact, she was no longer in that suffering mode at all and seemed genuinely happy. Soon after, this friend had twins, and suddenly her view of her husband and money (now that he was making more), and his mother, who babysat the twins twice a week while your friend was at this fantastic job, had altered. She began to praise these people, and you found it sickening, repellent. Where did this leave you? You couldn't change your tune; it would seem disingenuous. Plus, you still see the husband as cheap and the mother-in-law as a control freak—nothing has changed from where you stand. Basically, you move away, sniffing out another despondent friend. There's nothing here for you now.

Foul-Weather Friends

Women of all ages, from those in college to those in assisted living, are in search of female friends who echo their sentiments and resonate with them. The theory of homogamy, which I referred to in Chapter 1 in the context of female friendships based on similarities in race, age, education, social class, and religion (the standard basis of homogamy as it applies to marriage), extends to similar experiences. What threads the friendships together can be based on negative behaviors as well, such as two friends who found each other in a divorce support group exposing their bitterness toward their ex-husbands. When it comes to the glittering prizes of life, women congregate, despite undercurrents of envy, jealousy, and competition in the relationships—all three are fodder for the misery lover, and they manifest in several areas.

Lifestyle

At the top of the heap is what we aspire to in our capitalistic, materialistic society. Women are drawn to those who are like them, and who echo their lifestyle and values. As Virginia, 32, who lives in Southern California and works for a nonprofit, told me:

> My friends and I all want the same things, and it's fine as long as we all have it. But when one person gets pregnant or engaged or moves into a mansion, it changes everything. I sort of move away from anyone's success. Maybe I'm a bit jealous.

Romance

What better reason for discontent and envy than when your friend is in love and you can't meet a soul? While this friend was alone, it was comfortable and she was there 24/7. Now you're on your own and you secretly hope her new squeeze dumps her. Reeba, 36, who lives in Ohio, where she works at a museum, can attest to such feelings:

I have a friend who is always alone. I was the one with the rotten boyfriend and she was the third wheel. I listened to how lonely she was and she listened to how disgusting he was. She just met someone, and I can't be happy for her; I eat popcorn alone on Saturday nights.

Workplace

Women frequently gather at their jobs to commiserate about sexism, tokenism, and unequal pay for equal work. However, the majority of women compete only with female colleagues in this environment, fostering covert rivalry. If one woman is promoted, the misery lovers among the group will ice her. For instance, Joy, 49, who works for a corporation and lives in Nevada, expected a promotion, only to learn it had gone to a younger colleague.

I have been here for over ten years and I doubt anyone understands the company better than I do. I have trained women older than this woman who got the position. We used to all have lunch and talk about the ugliness of this business, moaning about the men and the vacation schedule. Now she's ecstatic and won't be at those lunches, I'm positive of that.

Careers

Working women befriend one another and trade war stories about the life balance of husbands, houses, children, and careers. This works well until one of the women finds herself leaving her career, increasing her salary significantly, or making a major shift in the kind of work that she does—breaking from the mold. Once this happens, her misery lover will often end the friendship. For example, Laura, 46, who works as an accountant and lives in a Midwestern city, has made the decision to leave for a more creative field.

Neither my friends who don't work nor my friends who do work wish me well. It's really weird, as if I fit into a box, and once I left, no one had the energy for my new plan. I think all of my friends liked it when I complained about tax season and they complained about their lives. No one wants your good news.

Motherhood

The late Betty Friedan described motherhood as "the most reviled and revered profession." Women are competitive with other mothers over their brand of mothering (working moms versus stay-at-home moms) and their children's achievements. Those who struggle with their children in some capacity find it comforting to speak with a friend in the same predicament. However, once the situation improves for one and not the other, the still afflicted mother moves toward another troubled mother/child situation. Alicia, 41, who is a stay-at-home mother and lives in Pennsylvania, admitted that she cannot be around her friend whose son just received a scholarship to kindergarten. Now she prefers to speak to the mothers whose children were also turned down at this school.

We all try so hard as mothers that the idea that some kids get chosen and others don't just makes me sick. This friend and I were on the phone every night while we were waiting for the results, and now that her kid—my best friend's kid—got this, I can't stand it. If only they'd both gotten it or neither had. If neither had, we'd be able to talk about how lousy it is forever. Instead, I have to talk to the other mothers whose kids also lost out.

Beauty and Age

From the time we are in grade school we know who the pretty girl is, the popular girl versus the wallflower. In a society that rewards beauty and youth, women choose attractive friends but can be jealous and envious of them at the same time. Ageism for women is at an all-time high, and women band together over this and are also divided on the approach. Some will opt for plastic surgery and cosmetic procedures and will lie about their age, while others have decided against this route. Consider Maureen, 34, who is an actress and lives in a Southern city. She is keenly aware of her looks, her age, and who wishes whom well.

I am always conscious of how other women perceive me and who my true friends are. When I get a part, I know who to call and tell my good news. When I don't get a part, I have another set of friends who will be there for me. Being over thirty, I also see younger women coming up and I'm competing against them. I admit, I'm friendly to them but I don't wish them success until I get what I think I deserve. So there's not much trust anywhere, and I don't share my good news so often, and I don't let any of the young actresses know how I feel about them—that I'd be happy to see them fail sometimes.

Sour Grapes

Although relationships between misery lovers seem idyllic at first, they also can evoke our narcissistic tendencies. Things can get uncomfortable when one friend moves on and the other remains in the phase that first brought the two women together. In the 2002 feature film *Crush*, starring Andie Mac-Dowell as Kate, three single, forty-something friends commiserate over their love lives. All is well until MacDowell's character falls for her former student, and her two friends are not only jealous but become manipulative in their quest to preserve life as it was.

As the story unfolds and Kate's life becomes richer, idolspizing (more on this in Chapter 6) kicks in; her friends seem unable to bear her happiness, and actually celebrate when it ends prematurely. According to a study conducted by Turner, Hogg et al., each of us is defined by a "personal identity," which is based on a person's singular traits, while "social identity" is about a person's belonging to a group. When we are with misery lovers, our personal identity appears secondary to our social identity; everyone needs to be comparable for the relationship to succeed. That is, unless the friends are willing to regroup and to rewrite the basis of the relationship once one of the friends has a sunnier story. Consider Dora, 37, who works in retail and lives in the Northeast and had a broken engagement two years ago. Afterward, she avoided happy occasions and only wanted to be with women who were as miserable as she was.

I had been engaged for six months when my fiancé told me it wasn't going to work. I was devastated and couldn't face any of my friends. Except the ones who were really in pain; then it was okay. So I hung around with one friend who was always lonely and depressed. We would go to the movies on Saturday nights, and it was really awful. We'd talk about why we didn't have the lives we were supposed to have. But I missed my fiancé and wanted to be with him. Saturday nights with a depressed girlfriend worked until I decided to get my life in order. I went online and met a few guys and began to date. I moved to a new store and I joined a gym. Meanwhile, this friend had a fit. She had actually introduced me to her lonely hearts club—a bunch of women who were so angry they were alone. It almost showed me how to make my life better, to not become like them. So I dated and dated and finally met someone really nice. That's when this friend made it clear that she and her friends didn't want me around anymore.

Filling the Void

What makes it all the more painful when the misery lover goes her own way is that there has been a heavy dose of intimacy in these relationships. In fact, over 70 percent of my interviewees felt that the misery lover was the one with whom they had spent the most time and with whom they had shared the most revealing information. The schism that the misery lover causes leaves her friend in great pain. Meanwhile, for the misery lover herself, who moves on, there is a chance to meet new unhappy friends, which she appreciates and thrives on. Consider Ashley, 36, who works in public relations and lives in the Southwest. Part misery lover, part mirroring friend, she decided to join AA after years of defending her alcohol abuse. This meant a break with some close friends and a search for replacement friends.

Part of why I wouldn't admit I had a drinking problem is because I drank with my best friends. It's something we'd done together for years and I didn't want to give it up. I knew enough about AA to know that I couldn't be in my old haunts doing my old stuff. I didn't want to lose these friends, who drank exactly like I did, and I couldn't imagine what I'd do on those drinking nights. Although we all drank, it was hurting me, while they could handle it. That's when I knew I had to be strong enough to do this alone. When I told my friends, they acted as if I'd let them down and denied that I had a problem. So there wasn't any support anywhere once I wasn't doing what we all did together. One friend acted like I was a turncoat.

Because I'm such a needy person, which I admit, I looked for women who were like me at AA and were just as confused and angry. I purposely went two towns away to start fresh, and when I listened to everyone, I decided to be with the women who were complaining the most. And it works; already we are talking about how, to the outside world, we looked fine and held our drink—and one woman abused painkillers—and how life has been hard for us. But we each knew deep down we had a problem, and that's why we became friends so fast. I keep thinking I'll go back to the old friends once I have this under control, but I'm not so sure it will be the same, since I can't do what they do, and we all know it. I doubt they want me back anyway, since half the time we talked about how bad life is, and how it's only okay if we're drinking.

What is interesting about Ashley's interview is how she gravitated toward women in AA who reflected her worldview and yet was able to make a healthy break in terms of her drinking. So while she has made a move to preserve herself, her take on female friendship has not been affected by this. Oftentimes the misery lover will give up a group of friends, or a friend, in search of those who reflect her present situation. While the friend left behind is understandably hurt, the friend who moves on continues her pattern, almost as if the friend is fungible as long as the next discontented friend is on the horizon.

The idea of being close to a female friend appeals to us from the time we're small girls, and there is a sense of security in these friendships. The connection is so revered that nothing can feel more damaging than to have a dearth of close friends. Young women depend upon their friends for an emotional foundation as well as to share interests, and so the friendships become critical.

Whatever adversity prevails with the misery lover, several approaches can be considered:

Loser/Loser. It is compelling to become attached to a friend because you both suffered a loss or disappointment.

Marcella, 36, has a troubled 14-year-old son. When she meets a mother at school whose son is known to be bad news, she befriends her. Not only does she feel that she's not alone, but her son looks better now.

Organic Connections. Although you've worked out at the same health club for years, it isn't until you confide your story to the woman in your locker row that you realize how parallel your lives are.

Nancy, 37, is under the care of a fertility specialist and has told no one in her family of her frustrations in trying to become pregnant. When her best friend introduced her to a colleague who has the same problem, the two women related at once. It's as if they've always known each other.

Schemes and Manipulations. Usually you keep your Machiavellian plans to yourself, but this one friend has confided a big secret, and you decide to exchange confidences. Dinners and luncheons ensue to tell each other all of your woes.

Nina, 41, is sleeping with her boss, and her best friend is having an affair. When Nina's friend's lover leaves his wife for her, it's infuriating and Nina has to pull away. She can't tolerate that her friend has gotten what she wants with her married man while her boss still buys his wife flowers.

Marginalized Women

Some women say they have friends who cling to each other *because* of their despondency. This makes sense, because according to a study by Seeley, Garner et al., "Circle of Friends or Members of a Group," women care more about relationships with other members of the group than about what the group stands for per se (unlike men, who identify *both* with the group and with the friendships that form within the group). When it comes to misery lovers, the thought of a collection of women suffering under the same roof, be it a divorce group, a concerned mothers' group, or a congregation of single women, is rewarding. Another scenario is when the misery lover's radar is up and she seeks out the unhappiest member of the PTA or an all-female reading group. To complicate matters, women say that when there is a leader who is also a misery lover, she can be divisive, and factions may evolve among peers. Amy, 48, a physician living in Pennsylvania with four children, illustrated this.

The mothers make it worse, and I'm sorry sometimes that I try to participate. It's as if they only like it when there's a problem. I'm unpopular because I don't have any problems with my kids or the school. So when I show up for these events, it's crazy. There's a line down the middle of the room and one side has all these complaints about the physical aspects of the building—it's an old school. The other mothers worry about their kids and sex and rock 'n' roll. Since I have no issues, I have an easy time with all of it, but I'm not very popular, and if I smile, they practically throw me out of the room. No one there finds things to be okay. And if they do, they'll be as unpopular as I am. Once I made a negative comment and two moms called me that night to explore it further.

In the beginning, the misery lover can handle the expectations implicit in female friendships. Her search for closeness motivates her to go the distance, and a leader who is also a misery lover is always open to new friendships. Yet she is also susceptible to the downfall of a friendship because her eagerness is so specific, meaning as long as the chips are down, she's there. This is how it has played out for Monica, 40, who moved to a small town in the Southwest after her divorce and recently lost her job in a restaurant. She decided to join a female bowling team to meet a few women.

I met a woman who was also divorced and unemployed in this bowling league—she ran the league. We became friends really fast and did so much together. It made me feel less alone and less like I'd made so many mistakes. She'd listen to my sad story and she'd make me feel better. She had some odd stuff in her life, too, but I was the one carrying on. Since my mom and sisters didn't want to listen, it was helpful to have her around. This went on for almost a year, and then I met a guy. It was like she no longer wanted to be with me, and she and a few other women on the team told me he was a bad guy. Then I actually got banished when he and I moved in together. It was too much good luck for my bowling friends, who wanted to drown their sorrows in their beers. I was really hurt. I want to make friends in this place, and I thought they'd be my friends. But what can I do?

Dire Straits

In her *Newsweek* column "My Turn," on March 31, 2008, Carla Drew addressed how alone she felt when she suffered a miscarriage. In her piece, "A Sisterhood of Suffering," Drew described how women are linked by miscarriages. Although hesitant to reach out to her friends when she miscarried, Drew was comforted by women she hardly knew who had had the same experience, and considered this an act of friendship. As several women have confided, it is the toughest times that render the most compassionate friends, as long as they have had the same exposure.

Lillian Rubin notes in her book *Just Friends* that friends are accepting of each other when there isn't change, or when they are both changing in the same way. It is when friends grow in different directions that the friendship is affected. Although women dread the fact that life experiences can have a negative or a positive effect on friendship, what we have witnessed in these interviews is a woman's choice to go with happiness and risk the friendship that doesn't support her good fortune and turn of events. Thus, in spite of the level of commitment, being a misery lover does not ensure security in a female friendship. Jessie, 49, who lives in upstate New York, has been quite fortunate in business and is ready for a set of friends who have more money and better social connections than her old crowd. She herself is part misery lover, part user, and a former doormat, who hopes to change her course.

I am deliberately stopping the friendships where I get off on everyone's bad times and rotten endings. I'm now making money after all these years building my business. So I don't want to be with people with problems anymore. I want a boyfriend who is a rich winner and I want women friends who can invite me to the right parties. Is this so wrong of me? I sat around for years and consoled everyone who had a bad time of it—my friends were always upset, always crying about something, and I lapped it up. I didn't know anyone who didn't wake up with a bad day ahead of her, and it got tiring. I kept thinking it was because we were poor. I kept thinking, If only I could make some money and get out of here, and then I did. My best friends were a sad bunch: One was widowed, one was beaten by her husband, one had a kid on drugs . . . No one knew anyone who was happy or successful. It was a drag, and I was right there with them. Now I want to be with women who are glamorous and superficial, and I will smile right back, like I mean it.

These old friends are very pissed off. They say that I'm abandoning them, and maybe I am. They're jealous that I've moved to the next town—a better town—and they're pissed that I'm trying hard to make new friends. They've also left me and don't invite me to anything anymore, and I know they talk about me. But do I want to do Tupperware parties and dinners at the local bar? Isn't that why I worked day and night, to escape this? So in the end, it's just because we were the same that we were friends, that we all hated everything so much. Deep down I'm not like that, and I know it now. I've broken free, and nothing can stop me.

Most misery lovers, like the mirroring friend, buy into the idea that a common link is the foundation of friendship. Another school of thought comes from our culture, in which we are raised to believe that as good girls, if we do the right thing, naturally the reward will follow. When translated into female friendships, there's a sense that unconditional giving to a friend, similar to what mothers do for their children, will bring about the right result.

The irony here is that the misery lover devotes herself to the relationship and hopes to be highly respected for her endeavor, but she isn't committed to a happy friend, only a miserable one. Researchers Clark and Ayers found that women are more intimate than men, maintaining closeness and expecting affection in return (something men don't look for). But this dedication among misery lovers is skewed, as we have seen. It's consistent with how women operate, but many of these friends leave when the sun shines for her once pathetic friend. It's little wonder that over 70 percent of the women interviewed for this chapter were disappointed and shocked when they found that their misery lover didn't want to celebrate their optimism or joy. Thirty percent of the women with whom I spoke said they knew at a certain stage in the friendship that it was best not to divulge all their good news if they wanted this friend to stay. As their lives improved, they became less than honest and open like they'd been in darker times. In this way, they managed to hold on, and the friendship, if it survived, became more superficial.

Diminishing Returns

Why are you a recipient of the misery lover's affection?
Women find this type of friend when their self-esteem is low and they are in pain. At this juncture, they find it pacifying to be with someone who is invested in their drama.

Why does it take the friend several "icy" episodes with her misery lover to realize the friendship is now unfulfilling?
Most women are deeply involved in their female friendships and do not want them to fail, despite that the relationship is in a rocky place.

When do you face the input/output equation in your friendship with the misery lover?
Over 80 percent of the women I interviewed realized that their friend did not support their turnaround. Twenty percent felt the friend was jealous and would get over it. When this happens, most women feel it's too much negativity and stop seeking the misery lover's friendship.

Endless Misery

If you are a misery lover, do you always find new friends and repeat your pattern?
Finding fresh prey satisfies you and makes you feel as if you count. It is only once you find your own happiness that you stand a chance at reinventing yourself.

Can you really reinvent yourself and steer away from this attitude?

You will have to work hard to break the pattern, but if you are also part mirroring friend, part sharer, part authentic friend, or part sacrificer, these styles of friendship will contribute to your moving away from your negative behavior.

Are you sometimes envious of someone who's having a modicum of happiness?

You may not have worked hard enough on yourself as an individual and on your own talents and strengths. Once you begin to do this, you will end up feeling less inclined to worry about your friend's sorrow or happiness and will focus on your own.

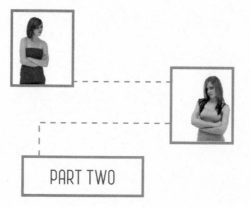

PART TWO

Those We Ditch: Trial by Fire

FIVE

The User: Self-Serving Friends

X Is your friend overly interested in your lifestyle or status?

X Does she work your crowd, attaching herself to your friends?

X Does she insinuate herself into your life?

X Is she nosy and intrusive?

X Do you feel slightly uncomfortable confiding in her for fear it might come back to haunt you?

When your friendship plays out this way, you have a user for a friend.

"From the time we were kids in this all-female household, I knew that I should have friends who were smart and ambitious and whom I'd do well to know," confessed Tina, 41, who works in finance and lives in Washington State. "My mother didn't work, but she would have been great at any kind of career, and she viewed her friends as her job. That meant she planned luncheons, bridge games, and shopping excursions. She used one friend for her big house and one friend for her driver and one friend for her housekeeper who cooked. She put lots of time into being the organizer, but her friends had to have something to aid the plan. I have gravitated toward women who are the same as I am at work and among the mothers I know through my kids.

"If someone can do something for me, especially with my long work hours, why not? My mother still does this now with her friends in Florida. I don't think anyone feels used, because everyone is being practical about how they do it. I see that my sisters do it too, with their friends, and it's not mean-spirited—it's just easier to fit with these women and so they're my friends."

The **user** stands alone in how every step she takes is purposeful and deliberate. Using a friend comes in all flavors: in a workplace situation, when it comes to social standing or meeting a man, or in terms of mothering and children. This friend can be enticing and charismatic and knows how to wheedle her way into one's life and firmly entrench herself. She also has a hidden agenda and, to this end, considers what is best for her. The conflict is that she's very appealing (more on this in Chapter 7, "The Trophy Friend"); there is a sense that the friendship is attractive enough to keep it intact, as frustrating as it can be. Women describe their friendships with a user as lacking a pure center, but admit to hoping it will improve somehow and therefore hanging in.

This type of friend enters the arena so early that by grade school women report having known a self-serving friend. Women also admit to having been one themselves on occasion. Although she exhibits shades of the leader, the doormat, the mirroring friend, the trophy friend, the frenemy, and even the sacrificer, the user is more self-absorbed and self-centered than other types of friends.

How Self-Serving Is This Friend?

Your neighbor invites you to a Sunday brunch for her cousin who just moved halfway across the country for her new job and knows no one in town. Since you have been in this situation, you quickly offer to bring the dessert and suggest a few women who might want to come. When introduced to this woman, you immediately feel that you could become friends, and you make a point of introducing her to the other working mothers and giving her your card. Soon enough, you are spending more time on the phone with this new "friend" than you do with your own sister, and you ask her and her children over one weekday evening for dinner. The friendship is established, and whatever she asks about people in your hometown, you are open and honest. Soon after, on a Saturday night, you invite her to join you and your husband with your two best friends and their husbands. In this environment, you observe how she makes a great effort to engage the other two women. That night when you return home, your husband mentions that she's a social climber, and you defend her, despite what you observed.

Several weeks later you learn that this new friend has offered to host the cocktail party for your children's grade at her home, although you told her you had hoped to do it for your child's sake and to prove that working mothers have time for such events. You also learn that she has put your two best friends on her committee but not you. When you confront her, pointing out that

*without your seal of approval, she would have none of this, she
says she isn't sure what you're referring to, that she was chosen for
her merits. Who would believe you if you confided in anyone
that this woman had used you?*

As evidenced in the synthesis above, the user is easily identifiable, and yet when we find ourselves sandwiched between
those who fall for her moves and the user herself, it can be a
slow-dawning and elaborate exit—*if* we exit. What is remark-
able about the user is the many ways in which her behavior
manifests itself. Eventually, according to my pool of interviewees, the user hones her skills for sniffing out her quarry.

Are You Being Used?

Consider Vicky, 50, who does volunteer work and lives in a
Southern state, and who can identify a user from afar.

Both my husband and I have made money and are charitable.
After a while people really glom onto you. I thought at first the
women just wanted to be my friend and I was so friendly, but now I
pay attention to what they say. If someone wants to be with me for
what it can do for them, I stay away. I know women like me, but
they also hate me for my good fortune. Women will act like your
friend, wondering what you can do for them. You end up learning
who your true friends are. I had this one friend and I thought it was
about me—that she chose me. But it was about whom she could
meet through us, tickets she could get to events and invitations to
parties. I was so hurt and upset. Ever since then, I've been more
careful.

So I get to know these women now who chase me down, and I ask myself, Does this person really want to be my friend, or is it for what's in it for her? Is it our position in the community that makes me attractive? And these supposed friends aren't going to stick by you in bad times; that I know. It's about what you or your husband can offer and how you're known.

Similar to Vicky in terms of women befriending her for her status is Constance. For Constance, 45, who lives in the Pacific Northwest, where she recently remarried and sold her business, there is also a not-so-distant memory of when she had the need to ask friends for favors.

I remember what it was like for me when my husband left me and I was working two jobs to support my girls. Some of my friends dropped me and said to stay away, either because I was single or because I no longer lived their kind of life. I called one friend whom I thought I could count on since we'd been such close friends, traveling with our kids and doing holidays together as families. I asked her if she could help us find a house to rent since she was a broker and she said no, flat out. She wanted nothing to do with me. I was down and out, and I admit, I was using connections from when I was married. I had no choice; I had to ask for favors.

Now, all these years later, I'm married to someone who is quite well known and people flock to me, even the ones who dropped me. The friend whom I asked to help with housing is nice again—nicer than ever before. I'm in a higher circle and she's looking to be friends; she's all over me. I haven't forgotten how she was when I was in trouble and I asked her for help out of necessity. What's she asking for? Because she's social climbing? I avoid those people; I don't want to have anything to do with them.

In her study "The Structure of Adult Friendship Choices," Lois M. Verbrugge states that "same-status people are very likely to choose each other as friends" because their perception of the world is similar. This "homogeneity basis" that she describes is familiar to us by now, and applies to several types of female friendships. Yet when this hypothesis is applied to the user, it means she seeks someone who serves her purpose *and* is similar enough. The user might intentionally seek out a friend of a higher class because this woman's lifestyle is a fantasy of hers, but she's clever enough to offer something in return. So while Verbrugge finds that "the less similar a pair of adults are, the less likely they are to become friends," a user who aspires to what the more fortunate friend has in terms of class or status works out an angle. For instance, Charley, 40, who lives in South Carolina and recently began teaching in a private school, was briefly reunited with her user.

Since my divorce, I've fallen on hard times. A lot of friends who used to come to my parties dropped me, and that hurt. But recently I ran into this old friend who now has more social standing than ever and whose husband has done so well. She wanted something from me, clearly, since I'm now beneath her as a single woman who had to sell her big house and get a job. Finally I figured it out: She wanted her son to get into the school where I teach. She also knew I work part-time in the admissions office. So after a few lunches and e-mails, she asked me what I could do. I definitely went to bat for her, because it was a chance, I thought, to get back the life I'd lost—so maybe I was using back on some level. And she did invite me to her parties for a short time. In the end, I couldn't get her son into the school. He really didn't have the grades, and there was no money she could throw at it that would make a difference to this place. It's more about academics, which seems honest.

So the friend dropped me a second time, since she couldn't use me to her advantage. I think this time I'll stay away. I was used years ago, when I had the life and she wanted to be a part of it, and again, for her kid. I know now that the friendship means nothing, and the chance to use the friendship works for her.

Our Mothers' Voice

In her book *Of Woman Born: Motherhood as Experience and Institution,* the poet Adrienne Rich reminds us of how powerful the role of the mother is and how mothering can change our society. As I mentioned earlier, our mothers' influence looms large; they have taught us how to communicate and interact with other women.

Did Your Mother Teach You to Use a Friend?

When it comes to the user, often the mother has been one herself or is well aware of the syndrome. And this, combined with the mother's relationship with the daughter, affects the daughter's need to be self-serving or not self-serving. As Dr. Claire Owen remarks, "What kind of rapport you've had with your mother and sisters will be reflected in how you feel about other women and what you expect from the relationships."

Consider Natalie, 39, who works in investment banking

and lives in a suburb of Boston. She and her mother share the view that self-serving relationships are expedient.

I am very careful who my friends are and how they reflect upon me. I worked my way up the ladder, and I don't want to miss a thing. When I was a kid, I always felt like I was missing out and I refuse to let it happen again. My sister is also someone who has worked hard to be where she is socially and with work. Sure, we've made it clear who we want for friends, but so what? My mother did this too. My mother taught us to be very conscious of whom we associated with and who our friends were. So I'm very aware of whom I spend time with, how it can help me and how it affects me.

I decided to rent a summer place in a resort where some powerful women live. I got myself invited to the parties, and I feel I've furthered my career and social life. It sure beats being someplace where no one is known. So what if friendships are about getting ahead? My mother would say that it's a waste of time if you can't get anything from a friendship. She also made me feel on edge, like I wasn't doing well enough at school or socially, and this has really affected me. My sister would say the same, and our mother would be annoyed with us if we didn't operate her way.

Juliana, 35, who works in a small business and lives in a suburb of Detroit, has been hoping to find a group of friends based on her family history.

My mother always tried to make me be "friends" with my sister. She emphasized how important it was that we be close. But she also favored me, and I viewed my sister as someone who wasn't my style and someone who didn't want what I wanted.

I couldn't help my mother out when it came to my sister, and my mom had to get over it since my sister and I had nothing in common. What I did instead was become the go-to person in our suburb, which made my mother happy enough, despite the fact that my sister and I didn't come through for her by being close friends.

Basically, I used my place in the family as a way to find the crowd I wanted. I am very ambitious and have done well at work. My mom approves of this—she wishes my sister would do it too. My husband knows how I feel socially and about money and has followed my lead. I've now got a group of women friends who have social ties and lead a life like ours. That's what I wanted, and I went after it. I don't think about my friends, Is this one nice, is this one smart, is this one a good person? I think, Is this the crowd I want to be with—and the answer is yes. And I don't waste time worrying about how it didn't work out with my sister. It's better I work on what has good results.

Opportunistic Mothers

What I found in my research for my book *Tripping the Prom Queen: The Truth About Women and Rivalry* is that the seeds of envy, jealousy, and competition are often planted by our mothers, and that the mother's take on these emotions offers the model for their daughters and their own female friendships. If a mother is envious of her friends, and rivalrous, then this is what her daughter has learned to do or not to do. Claudia, 46, a nurse practitioner in South Florida, recalled how her mother only befriended women in her hometown whom she considered socially acceptable within their working-class sphere.

It wasn't that we were so fancy but that everyone was going to college and was going to be able to make their own money. My mother raised us to think that we were special and that she was special even though she was working at the high school. That meant we were smart, good students, and were constantly reminded that had she had the chance, she'd have had a real career. I think she was bitter she didn't get to do more, and maybe that's why her attitude was that friends had to have some merit. They couldn't just be fun but had to be able to do something for her, for us.

I think she could be jealous, too, if one of her friends inherited money or had a son who got a scholarship to college. When that stuff happened, and it did, she definitely thought, When will my day come? So her friends had to do little things—one of her friends gave her discounts at the local clothing shop where she worked; another friend's husband owned a used-car dealership, so we could get a car cheaper. And she would help her friends' kids at the high school if they needed something, if she could. As her daughter, I'm always conscious of my friends, who is who and who can do something in some way.

Telltale Signs of the Self-Serving Friend

Although it may not be obvious at first, eventually the friend who uses her friends to suit her own needs is recognizable. There are myriad ways in which a friend does this, and to greater and lesser extents. The underlying pattern is what I address in the following breakdown.

The Instant Friend

From the moment you meet, this woman is available, willing, and bighearted—as long as it promotes her plans. Your life is hers, your children are of great interest, as is your career, and she is in a rush to know more.

For Carole, 49, who lives in St. Louis, where she is a television producer, and who has one daughter, the instant friend seemed a savior.

I met this friend in Europe years ago when our kids were in school together. We were both married to men who worked at a corporation and she thought we needed to be friends in this foreign country. First she was all over me, and planned all our time together. Then she began to tell me all her troubles, and I had to listen. I had to be her friend who sympathized; she had no one else. She wouldn't let go of me because she had to have me as a friend. She was very needy, and I became the sounding board.

The "It's All About Her" Friend

The scenario is that you offer something she has to have. The recipient of this kind of friend reports feeling used, since once the basis for the friendship changes, the friend loses interest.

Faith, 33, who works in marketing and lives in Northern California, found that her friend wasn't sincere.

I met this woman at work and she had an older brother and wanted us to meet. Her brother and I began dating, and I thought it was going to work out. The real story was that he'd been jilted by his fiancée and his sister was desperate to find someone to take his mind off it. When I thought the relationship was getting serious, it was just this guy getting over his pain and his sister setting me up to help him out. I was brokenhearted when he said he wasn't ready, while she thought I'd served a purpose.

The Über Manager

This kind of friend doesn't jump in but takes her time before you realize you are an instrument in her plan. She forges what seems to be a bona fide friendship and then begins to self-serve. By then you care about her, and just when you're about to let go, she reels you back in.

As Cynthia, 47, who works in fashion and lives in Maine, recalled, she began to avoid her friend once she understood her behavior.

I valued this friendship and then I figured out what she was up to, that she wanted a friend once she moved here and was lonely. She was very entertaining before she fell apart and wanted my assistance. So I was there for the easy part, and then I found out she had to have real help, that she was a neurotic mess. I stuck around because she begged me to, and I got caught up in all her troubles. It was awful. Finally I found a way to escape.

The Friend Who Considers Only Herself

Although you delude yourself that this friend has your best interests at heart, the truth is she only thinks of you as it pertains to her. This affects minor and major situations equally, from making a dinner date that she'll break if something better comes along to being her priority, depending on what you bring to the table.

Pat, 39, who works as an accountant in a Southern town, admitted to making plans and breaking them, based on how her calendar shapes up.

I usually say yes to every invitation and then start shuffling things around in order of importance. I'll send a nice e-mail, saying I'm so sorry, I double-booked, which is true, or I didn't realize . . . whatever. This way I keep my options open and my friends stand by me. Sure, they might be annoyed or inconvenienced, I might be known as someone who does this, but in the end, it's okay.

The High-Gear Friend

This user is lively and enticing (more on this in Chapter 7), and women often sign on unwittingly, because the energy feels good, initially. Once the user puts her plans into effect, it is annoying or worse, but her vitality may keep you attached.

Lauren, 48, who is a college administrator in upstate New York, believes that women befriend her because of her husband's involvement with the media.

My husband is powerful and can make things happen. He can get things in the news and on the air and has access to social events. People want that. Some women want to be close to me because of the kind of life he and I lead, and these women, the ones who have a motive, are always the most fun. They're peppy and friendly, and I have to be cautious. I try to wear antennae, but mostly I give in to the good parts of the women, though I know I'm being used.

What occurs with the user are scenarios in which she achieves her goals and is satisfied, while her friend, who has been a provider, can feel duped. And yet, as attested to by Carol and Lauren, there is a conscious decision to be with this friend on an ongoing basis. This decision is made despite the fact that trust isn't of great importance to a user. In her study "Dynamics of Relationships," Susan D. Boon describes trust as an "expectation," and explains that the "partner" will be compelled to consider the friend's "best interests." As we see, this is not the determination of a user/self-serving friend.

Ego Gratification and the User

In order to have healthy friendships, women need to have enough ego to apply it to the relationship. Unfortunately, when a woman lacks this, the balance between her needs and her friends' needs is not clearly established—the user enters the scene and the less confident friend falls for her. According to Dr. Ronnie Burak, those with narcissistic traits put themselves ahead of others as a mechanism for dealing with their lives. "Either these women were raised as princesses and the world revolved around them and they find ways as adult women to make sure their needs are met," remarks Dr. Burak, "or it's the opposite, and these women didn't get their needs met as young children and didn't get their fair share of love and nurturing. So they will use a friend to make things happen for them now that they missed before."

For example, Jennifer, 56, who works in sales and lives in a suburb of Chicago, described herself as being on high alert when it comes to her friends and her surroundings.

I'm always looking for beauty, and I choose my friends by how they adorn a room or what kind of places they will go to. I'm drawn to friends who look good and like attractive environments. My women friends aren't part of a group but are spread all around. What they have in common, however, is this search for the same things; they're beautiful people who can afford to be immersed in beauty. Sure, they'll use me to get to the beach in the summer and I'll use them for winter getaways. This feeds our egos and makes me happy. I don't waste anyone's time, and I don't allow anyone to waste mine. This is what I look for, and nothing else works. If someone wants plastic surgery or her house needs work, I'm all for it. We have to concentrate on what looks good because it feels good, and I'm used for my input in these cases. But in the end, I win because I don't sell myself short on seeking out what I have to have.

The Business of Friends

Jennifer's blatant narcissism reflects a society that sanctions the user. Andrea, 48, a single mother living in western Connecticut, where she runs a family business, recognizes her own use of her friends.

Everything I do is for business. My real friends are part of it too because I don't have the luxury of dividing my work friends from my social friends. I expect that if I put out for these friends, throwing parties and inviting both sets, it is so my name is known. If a friend makes a comment about this, then she doesn't have to do it my way. But I have to push to make things happen as a single mother. So I park myself with women friends who look good and act a certain way. If someone doesn't like it, she's out of my circle. It sounds heartless, but it's business.

While the user courts favor by being indispensable, she also may have a sense of entitlement. Steil, McGann, and Kahn define this as "a set of attitudes about what a person feels he or she has the right to." The person "expects" this as a member of a group and also as an individual. The egotistical friend is frequently able to rationalize her user behavior because she believes she is entitled to the result.

Self-Serving by Degrees

Although the user appears to be the friend to leave (along with a frenemy) when the gig is up, and a woman who realizes this can be quite indignant, the theory that no one is all bad definitely applies to this kind of friend. Besides, as we'll see, there are users who are completely comfortable with their schemes and so are not inclined to leave, but to perpetuate their role.

At the Top of the Game

Consider Adrienne, 32, who moved to a new town on the West Coast and immediately jumped into the social events at her daughter's school. She admitted that she charmed everyone, as she had in the past in her old haunts, and earned the role of leader.

Sure, I wanted to be involved for my daughter's sake, but everything about it was on purpose. I invited the mothers of the girls my daughter liked out to lunch. I worked the room at the parents' meetings because I wanted to find the right crowd. Then I convinced my husband that we should have a dinner party to get into the right group. But both my daughter and I benefited, and I have made friends from this plan. I always make sure to volunteer at the meetings, to give some of my time, and in exchange, I'm getting where I want to be. In fact, I'm in charge of two committees and am practically back where I started in my hometown. I don't need a real friend, who will go to the mall with me or listen to me at midnight when I admit my problems, but I need the social connections.

Saving Grace

Liz, 53, who works in Rhode Island, knows that her work friend "stole" her job as a supervisor after Liz mentored her and shared her knowledge. Today she uses that friend to ensure her own position.

I had been at this company for eight years and my colleague had been there for five. She was quite a bit younger and a good worker. We became close work friends, which I now realize was a mistake, and I taught her all I knew about the company. She was nice to me, but she had a plan. She told me about her mother's career and how she'd climbed the corporate ladder however she could. This friend was obviously self-serving; she believed in it. She learned my job and took it. I'd say she was never a friend and I was a fool to think otherwise. I'm still nice to her because we're in the same business, but I no longer tell her anything. I want people to think we're still friends and not that she used me. Maybe I'm starting to use her to prove I'm above it all and to make sure that she can't hurt me in the future. I'm in it because she started it, but I won't back off.

The Full Advantage

Similar to Adrienne is Wendy, 42, who works in fashion and lives in a Southern city. A sacrificer by nature, she puts the self-serving mode into action to advance herself at work.

This is such a cutthroat business that when I decided to try to rep from home, I had to have contacts who would support this. I'd always been happy to be there for a friend, to go the limit. Since most of my friends are work friends in my world as a single woman, I figured when the time came that I could ask them to do something for me, and get business that way. I really believe all those years of being the quiet one who did for her friends and said nothing but was accommodating has helped me to say, Now it's my turn. I use that to get business. I push hard because I have no other choice, and those who used me are on top of my list since I'm ready to use.

The Downside

In the feature film *27 Dresses*, Jane Nichols, played by Katherine Heigl, is not totally aware of how much of a user her younger sister, Tess, played by Malin Akerman, is. Tess not only gets engaged to the man Jane has a huge crush on, her boss, played by Ed Burns, but she announces to Jane that Jane's best friend, Casey, played by Judy Greer, will have to be in her bridal party since Tess has no friends of her own (implying that her beauty and personality keep other women away). At this point, Tess's self-serving techniques are taken too far, and Jane, who has put up with her sister's act for years, finally blows the whistle. Nonnie, 33, a dental hygienist, recently chose to cut off a friendship for similar reasons.

I became friends with this woman on a biking trip and later introduced her to my boyfriend and his friend, for a double date. Afterward she told me that my boyfriend was more her type than his friend. But she was so friendly and accommodating to me that I was too stupid to realize she was after him and would find a way to do things with us, like go to a movie or on a hike on a Saturday. Once I understood, I left.

Repositioning Ourselves

Ronnie, 38, a stay-at-home mother living in Arizona whose husband travels a great deal for work, has recently realized she can be self-serving when the occasion arises, despite her doormat mentality.

After all these years of being the quiet one and taking on my best friends' messes, I decided to hunt for a part-time job. I think because I'd been so meek and mild, listening to everyone's misery, I felt it was time to use these friends for their connections. One of my closest friends is in the position to hire freelancers and I went straight to her and said, Do this for me. I'm waiting to hear back. But if she doesn't come through, I won't stop there. It's almost like I have something over these friends for listening to all of them spill their guts, and I plan to get myself somewhere with that.

Audrey, 59, who lives in Texas, is the mother of four. She told me that she has been a user all her life. Her full disclosure saves the day.

I make sure I'm with friends who know how I operate, and my second tier of friends are those who are my victims. My good friends know I'm in it for the social set and also for what someone can do for me or one of my kids or grandchildren. I make no bones about it, and that's why the friendships last. No one has to guess what I'm doing or what I want. It's all very obvious, and I've no regrets. I know I am a good friend, as I see it should work.

The Losses

Although many women endure this type of suboptimal friendship for a period of time and are likely to find ways to have it work in their favor, once they do sever the relationship, they report a clean break.

For the 70 percent of women who are users or have been used, 30 percent decide to leave, echoing the professionals, who raise the issue of what genuine friendship is about and how we seek it. When it fails, there are several factors:

When are the user's actions too egregious?
Even if a friend forgives her user or feels she understands her, she can be turned off when the user's behavior borders on being harmful to the user herself or to another person.

Why is everything about this friend blatant and deliberate?

If she drops you once you've served her purpose, and you can't make any more excuses for her, there is no foundation for the friendship.

When does a friend who is used hit her threshold?

Because users are sophisticated in their self-serving methods, it could take years before an innocent friend has had her full. If there has been too much damage due to the user's game plan, the friend will walk away.

Profitable Endeavors

A healthy friendship can evolve between those friends who are self-serving, under the following conditions:

Both friends are at the same game and respect each other's strategies.

As long as the user/usee or user/user are aware of the self-serving parts of their friendship and they still appreciate each other, this can be satisfactory. No one feels taken advantage of, and rarely are feelings hurt; rather, there is a level of "mirroring" and mutual self-interest.

The players are bonded through worthy endeavors.

If the self-serving friend is in cahoots with other users, and their goals are common but not overlapping, this bodes well for the entire group. Several women described a clan of friends as women with self-interests. Yet the group does well because the members support one another; the cause and effect of their actions meets with approval.

The user has too much to offer to let her go.

If the advantages outweigh the disadvantages and the desire for the friendship justifies one's action, women will stay with their user. Other women who feel lonely and are skeptical of new friendships rationalize the friendship and stay, looking beyond the behavior.

SIX

Intimate Frenemies: Idolspizing

✗ Have you confided in your friend only to find your secret spilling everywhere?

✗ Is she capable of undermining you, and at the same time seeming to care?

✗ Does she comment often on how prominent her other friends are?

✗ Does she applaud you for your success and resent your success at once?

✗ Do you sense she is jealous and/or envious of an aspect of your life, while supportive elsewhere?

If so, you are in the hands of a frenemy.

"I met this woman ages ago and I wanted to be friends. I introduced her to all my friends and showed her around since she was new in town and I'd been there since college," began Emma, 35, who lives in St. Paul, where she is a nurse practitioner. "I knew more people than she did, and so I was very open and inviting. I introduced her to my boss at this temp agency, and she ended up temping where I did to make some extra money. By then she was making these remarks about my looks, that I was thin, that I had all the friends, that I always got what I wanted. Still, I trusted her and introduced her to a man whom she knew I liked, and it was as if I didn't exist. She brownnosed into the group that he was friendly with, and any connection I had there sort of disappeared. It was really weird the way she maneuvered it, so that she could exclude me. That seemed to be a big part of it—that she had what I had and that I was eased out. I had to hear about it through a mutual friend.

"Finally, she got the guy I liked and they lived together for a few years. That's when I felt the most betrayed because she knew how I felt about him. Recently I heard she's made a big name for herself and that she's going to be in town, but I doubt I'll ever speak with her again."

The **frenemy** is the dark side of the user, with manipulation an underlying factor in these negative relationships. Many times her act is refined, unlike that of blatant enemies on the schoolyard during our grade school days. While there are facets of the leader, the mirroring friend, the user, and the trophy friend in the frenemy, she rarely has a conscience and always has a designated program in mind. Although it is apparent why and when one should walk away from this kind of friend, cultural messages, oddly enough, ramp up our view of frenemies. This gives tacit approval for the emotions and passive-aggressive behaviors that accompany the relationship. The deed, in such situations, can prove cataclysmic and the range striking. The question for those who have a frenemy or two in their lives is what level of toxicity is tolerable?

The Dangerous Zone

I purposely titled this chapter "Intimate Frenemies" because a frenemy frequently ingratiates herself to a friend, and the relationship might feel close at first. According to the *American Heritage Dictionary, intimate* means "pertaining to or indicative of one's deepest nature." A frenemy, according to the *Chicago Sun-Times,* is someone who is "a friend+an enemy," while Ninjawords defines frenemy as "someone who pretends to be your friend but is really your enemy." In this way, the intimacy is bogus, and one friend can hold something over the other. Or you start off in what appears to be a healthy manner, then this friend reveals her true feelings or exhibits signs of betrayal. One woman reported that a friend never returned a designer purse she'd loaned her. Another reported that a friend lifted her idea for a children's accessory line and passed it off as her own. A third discouraged her best friend from dating a certain man only so that she could date him.

These women can't help themselves—an opportunity is presented and the friendship becomes invisible. In any of these instances, the condition can be exacerbated if idolspizing has kicked in. Idolspizing, as described by Ann Hornaday in *The Washington Post,* is the "tricky emotion between idolizing and despising." When someone is a frenemy, they usually also engage in idolspizing (which worsens when one friend has what the other desires). There is an inherent lack of trust, even if the friend postures as trustworthy or sincere. Consider Danielle, 37, an attorney who lives in Pennsylvania. Her close friend turned out to be a frenemy who tossed her aside.

We were friends for years, really devoted to each other. Our older kids played together, and as couples we went to dinner and movies. We told each other a lot and went out of our way for each other—enough for me to think it was a real friendship. Then this friend started to make a lot of money, and we weren't fancy enough. I admired her work ethic and the payoff but hated her for being this way to us—and for her success. We aren't invited to the parties she gives now, and this made me hate her. She wasn't the same, but I wanted to still be in her circle, to be part of it. I know she's not a friend anymore so I might as well fake that I'm her friend, to get to go to her parties. I'm the pathetic one, I take the crumbs, but I can't stand that her life has turned out this way. It's strange how I've turned into an ugly person since she got ahead of me. I didn't know I could be this way—saying nasty things and acting unhappy for her happiness.

There are many ways in which this sort of friend enters our lives and also in which the frenemy herself materializes. A deeply troubling news story concerned the suicide of Megan Meier, 13, who was allegedly lured by her friend; her friend's mother, Lori Drew; and Ashley Grills, Drew's employee, by a fictional romantic interest, "Josh Evans," whom they devised on MySpace. According to P. J. Huffstutter's article "Frontier Justice in an Online World?," which ran in *The Seattle Times* on November 23, 2007, Megan Meier and Lori Drew's daughter were friends in elementary school and later "grew apart." After several weeks of communicating online, Huffstutter wrote, "Josh Evans" "abruptly turned on Meier and ended it. Meier, who previously battled depression, committed suicide that night." Thus a mother's influence, a friend's actions against a friend, and the fact that cyberbullying is now a part of our culture are the haunting themes of this tragic tale.

High-Octane Insincerity

On a lesser scale, but with repercussions nonetheless, are the day-to-day experiences with a frenemy. The majority of women expressed that these friendships had begun innocently enough but had become misleading, enveloped in an air of mistrust. This development occurs in the feature film *The Break-Up,* about a couple who decides to call it quits, starring Jennifer Aniston as Brooke and Vince Vaughn as Gary. Once this promising love relationship is on the rocks, Brooke's best friend, Addie, played by Joey Lauren Adams, comes to the rescue, supposedly. Addie is all too eager to lend an ear and offers more advice than is needed, but what makes her an idolspizer is how purposely wrong her advice is, undermining any chance that Brooke might have of being reunited with her boyfriend. Watching this movie, I wondered why Addie didn't wish the best for her friend and how she had the power to be so persuasive. Perhaps the two friends had a history of Brooke's being the winner who takes all. Perhaps it was satisfying to Addie that Brooke, pretty and desirable, was finally miserable and tormented, since Addie, saddled with children and a boring husband, secretly wished for Brooke's more glamorous life. Whatever Addie's motivation, it conjured up the adage "With friends like that, who needs enemies?"

The Pretend Cheerleader

Would it be better to declare your frenemy an archenemy and an outright betrayer? Most women say not, and so this identifiable pattern, found in those who idolspize despite its being counterintuitive to the rich, warm sense of female bonds, is one we encounter often enough. As psychotherapist Seth Shulman points out, women are discouraged from being close in these instances, and merely go through the motions. "Female friendship isn't nurtured, although women band together if the situation arises," Shulman remarks. "This means they do not always honestly support one another as friends, or know how to be friends."

Casey, 33, who lives in New York State and works in advertising, discovered how the true nature of a friend can surface when she got married.

I got engaged first, and my friend since we were kids was so jealous that she became obsessed with becoming engaged. She would vanish and then reemerge, and she was always talking about her wedding. This went on during my engagement and at my actual wedding. But she wasn't even engaged then, and as another friend pointed out, this is how this friend had been since she had a boyfriend—she wasn't happy for me but crazy jealous. I didn't want her attitude around me at my wedding, but what could I do when she was talking about how her nonexistent wedding would be? While she'd be devastated to know I think poorly of her as a friend, it's become too much work to be her friend when she isn't happy for me but wants what I have. So it's over. My wedding was the deal breaker because I saw her true colors. I knew better than to trust her; she's really not a friend anymore.

Similar to Casey is Audrey, 63, who remarried eight years ago after having been widowed. She lives in a retirement community in Arizona, where she recognizes that the women she's befriended are less than sincerely pleased for her.

Women hate me and also tip their hats to the fact that I remarried such a nice man and someone so good-looking. They know what it takes to meet a guy, but they won't be nice about it. These women have negative energy, one in particular, so I'm very guarded. I don't share anything with anybody and I just act friendly. That's how I've decided to be after watching one woman's group of single friends congregate around her husband as a potential mate when she became sick. These women hang over me, wishing me ill so they can pounce on my husband. They call themselves friends. This one woman stays my friend so she can find out about my life, my marriage, my health—all to her advantage. She'll bake and bring a pie over or she'll invite us to a party. I smile and act friendly, but she's not my friend.

Are You Hated for Your Happiness?

Women who are jealous and idolspize might simply be too unhappy themselves to offer the qualities that define satisfactory female bonding. Although Eric G. Wilson notes in his book *Against Happiness* that misery has merit and that possibly it is the human condition to be unhappy, it is nonetheless troubling to see that friendships fail when someone is wallowing in anguish. What makes it worse is the prevailing assumption that friends might be annoying, clinging, demanding, manipulative, but they won't do you in, when, in fact, a frenemy will do just that. Therefore, there is the glaring discrepancy between the actions of the frenemy and studies such as that

of Oswald, Clark and Kelly's "Friendship Maintenance: An
Analysis of Individual and Dyad Behaviors." Their work indicates that female friendships have not only more interaction,
support, and openness than do male same-sex friendships,
but more intimacy and acceptance as well. This is not what
transpired with Kay, 46, a nurse, who lives in a large city. She
feels that she had the support of her friends until she fell in
love.

As long as I was willing to sit around and complain about my
divorce and money, everyone was my pal. All of my girlfriends
were pissed off like me and we would console one another and
drink a lot of wine. Once I ended up with my college boyfriend, after kids and divorces and lots of bad times, no one seemed to care.
That's when I realized that a few of my friends wished me the
worst, and didn't want me to be okay, let alone pleased with things.
That was quite a blow.

I doubt I would have learned this about any of my friends if I
hadn't been through so much—if I'd stayed married or had fared
poorly after my divorce. It's finding happiness that makes everyone so insane. What a shame. I think there's enough money, love,
and happiness to go around that women shouldn't do this, but
they do.

The Sabotager

To take it a step further, there are those friends who not only
rejoice in your discontent, as documented above, but who will
also go out of their way to stir up a problem *and* then work the
situation to their advantage. As Olivia, 27, who works in retail

and lives in Kansas, described her "work friend," it was a friendship first and then a fight to the finish.

My friend and I began working in the company together and we became friendly fast. Then she got promoted. I didn't exactly report to her, but in a roundabout way I did. Then I was promoted, and moved to another department. I thought she'd be happy for me, since I was happy for her when she got her promotion. Instead, she made a fuss to our boss and made it very hard for me to transition into the new department. I was surprised since we'd always been friends. She tried to ruin it for me so I wouldn't have my new job or so I didn't seem qualified. Obviously she isn't my friend anymore, but I'll always be smiling when I run into her or on a company outing. I am hurt on two levels—one, because she was supposed to be my friend, and two, because women should stick together at work and she wouldn't do that. She's not the person I thought she was and it is a cold war now.

Celebrity Status

The attitude that female friendship is fraught with unhappiness is a staple of the media, observed in news stories, on television, in film, and in fiction. We are bombarded by catfights and intrigued by female competition when it comes to the lives of stars. A famous feud between celebrity writers Lillian Hellman and Mary McCarthy began in the late 1930s, according to Wikipedia, over ideological differences. Amazingly enough, close to fifty years later it was still festering, and when McCarthy announced on *The Dick Cavett Show,* "Every word

[Hellman] writes is a lie, including 'and' and 'the,'" Hellman filed a $2.5 million libel suit against her. Although the suit was dropped by the executors of Hellman's estate after she died in the early eighties, the episode created quite a stir in its day.

Today attention to celebrity women and their lives continues. Notable among these tales was that of Star Jones Reynolds's exit from *The View* in April 2006. According to Julia Savacool's article in *Marie Claire* in August 2007, Reynolds believed things went sour because the cohosts had changed over the nine years the show had been on the air. "It's like having a good girlfriend when you graduate college, then you get your dream job and she doesn't. In six or seven years, you might not be as close. That's what happened on the show," Reynolds explained the situation.

Another example of a famous woman and a friendship gone awry, with the media as backdrop, is that of Cherie Blair, the wife of Tony Blair, former prime minister of Britain, and her former aide, Fiona Miller. An article that ran in the *Daily Telegraph* on July 7, 2007, by Richard Alleyne, "Cherie Is Hypocritical and Naive, Says Aide," informed that one of Blair's "former, closest advisers" labeled Blair as being unable to take advice well during her husband's tenure as prime minister. According to the piece, Miller discussed Blair as someone who preferred "to cast herself as a victim of the press and other nebulous, evil establishment forces." The two women were once close, but, Alleyne wrote, "Miss Miller said that the ending of the friendship with the former prime minister's wife was a painful time, especially as Mrs. Blair tried to sack her."

For younger women, since 2006 there has been the opportunity to watch *The Hills,* a reality show that airs on MTV about women in their twenties who might or might not appreciate their friendship, depending on what the drama of the week is. The show takes place in L.A., where Lauren Conrad is seeking a fashion career. She and her three friends, Heidi, Audrina, and Whitney, spend time at restaurants and clubs, where they discuss relationships. When the 2007 season ended, Heidi and Lauren had stopped being friends; and to make matters worse, Lauren claimed that Heidi had put the word out that Lauren and an old boyfriend had made a sex tape.

Who Wore It Best?

That celebrity women, friends or foes, are compared to one another for looks, popularity, and how they wear a dress doesn't help the matter, and the regular feature "Who Wore It Best?" in *Us Weekly* definitely adds to the fray. In the August 27, 2007, issue, the magazine reported that 61 percent of the 100 people asked on L.A.'s Robertson Boulevard preferred Lauren Conrad, compared to 39 percent who preferred Sarah Michelle Gellar in the same dress. Mandy Moore at 52 percent won by a slim margin over Sophia Bush at 48 percent for their same attire, and Carmen Electra garnered 35 percent of the vote to Keri Lynn Pratt's 65 percent for their designer frock. The level of rivalry over a dress is only the tip of the iceberg, as celebrity women are scrutinized and set as examples when it comes to their friends, lifestyles, and romances.

The end of the friendship between Paris Hilton and Nicole Richie, who were costars on the reality television show *The Simple Life*, was fodder for the gossip pages. The schism of the starlets was reported on StarBlogs.net on April 20, 2005, in an article entitled "Paris Hilton and Nicole Richie Confirm Their Breakup." That the relationship was classified as a breakup, a word usually identified with romantic splits (referenced above in the film *The Breakup*), impresses upon us the weightiness of such a relationship. Hilton announced the friendship was "simply over," according to the Web site, yet the article described the women's feeling toward each other as "seething contempt," more the stuff of idolspizing than a solid friendship.

In the September 2007 issue of *Vanity Fair*, Nancy Jo Sales's piece on a group of young celebrity women and the men with whom they "hook up," "I'm with Her," detailed the tangled frenemyship among Paris Hilton, Lindsay Lohan, and Britney Spears. In writing about a young man whom Lohan dated, Sales wrote, "Lindsay might have taken up with Stavros to make Paris mad. Paris had him first." And she quotes one woman explaining, "Paris has done *horrible* things to Lindsay. . . . And still Lindsay will call her, saying, 'I want to be friends again.'" If this is worthy of a *Vanity Fair* article, we know that this enclave of young women has an impact. But what kind of model is this behavior for young women? Even if it is counteracted with such important messages as the one in Tina Fey's adaptation of Rosalind Wiseman's nonfiction book about female teenagers, *Queen Bees and Wannabes*, into the feature film *Mean Girls*? In theory we *know* how to be a loyal, trusting, dedicated, sincere friend, and how it feels to be in such a positive relationship, yet many times, it doesn't seem the right option. If a female is a "celebrity," at any age, in her hometown, it can conjure up more bad behavior, emanating from her and her cronies.

A Recurring Theme

Consider Diane, 45, who lives in a suburb of a Midwestern city, where she works full-time in finance. Her ability to idolspize has been altered by the fact that she is now idolspized herself.

I used to want what other people had, and I made no bones about getting in with the right crowd, the known crowd. I have always had friends for a purpose. One friend includes my son in every sports activity, and another friend carpools my girls to ballet. This is all useful since I have a heavy-duty job and my work schedule is demanding. But more important is that my kids are at the right schools and have the right friends. I've always wanted a moneyed life, and before I had it, I was the one who was jealous and secretly hated women who had a better time. I also had to have them as friends, and I made it a business to get that done. I was lucky and it happened for us; my husband has done well too. So I edged out the friends who couldn't do something for me, or weren't in the crowd I wanted to be with. I admit I made friends with people I didn't even like because they helped me socially. And I've tossed people aside who made me look like less. It's a job getting to this social level, and the friends I left behind hate me, I know it. They suck up to me because of my lifestyle, but I'm not interested.

Backstabbing

What Diane describes is a recognizable motive, and for her, celebrity status translates into a moneyed life and the chance to be the leader. When it comes to men as a prize possession, a story that caught the public's attention was the triangle of actresses Denise Richards and Heather Locklear and their mutual love interest, Richie Sambora. As Jeannette Walls reported on April 27, 2006, on Msnbc.com, the question of when Richards and Sambora became an item is critical to how the women's friendship dissolved. Richards and Locklear were neighbors in the San Fernando Valley, and Richards encouraged Locklear to file for divorce, according to Walls, who referenced *In Touch Weekly* for this information. Apparently a "pal" was quoted in the magazine saying that the friendship was over since "Heather thinks Denise is the worst kind of woman—a backstabber."

Celebrity women appear worthy of one another by virtue of being in a select "club" where there seems to be little need to hurt one another. When this proves to the contrary, it is viewed with great curiousity by others. For women everywhere, it is a troubling equation when a friend is someone who covets what you have, *and* is capable of befriending you as a means to an end, without any sincere feelings about the relationship. The friendship turns sour even as the women appear to be so close, reflecting each other in their looks and status, while competing for the glittering prizes: men, lifestyle, money, children, looks, and professional success. To top it off, one woman might be naive and genuinely shocked to learn she has been lured into imagining this woman is her friend. Most women in this position describe themselves as victims who cannot quite believe that this is happening to them.

Who Is Your Frenemy?

Constant idolspizing is depicted in the 2001 film *Me Without You*, starring Michelle Williams as Holly and Anna Friel as Marina. Two best friends from childhood to adulthood are typecast, Holly as the innocent, suffering one and Marina as the idolspizer whose narcissism keeps her from being an honest friend. When Holly falls for Marina's brother, Nat, Marina's nastiness escalates in her selfish efforts to keep them apart. The confusion for Holly is that Marina's actions and jealous nature are cloaked in the guise of winning friendship. As the years go on, what was once extreme rivalry has turned Marina into a frenemy rather than a genuine, if flawed, friend to Holly.

Consider Alice, 34, who works in sales and lives in Santa Fe with her daughter.

My best friend seems to care about me and my life, but mostly we talk about her and we do what she wants. I think she loves me and she hates me because her son has serious problems and my daughter just got a scholarship for grade school. But no one's life is perfect, and with this friend, my story doesn't count. She discounts both me and my daughter when she talks about people's accomplishments, as if we don't even exist. It's not easy to put up with her, and my husband always says, Why are you friends? I care about her even though she can be so wretched. I think she even wants my child to fail, that's how bad it is with her, how much she wants to win.

Another film worth mentioning at this juncture is *The Women*, based on the play by Clare Boothe Luce, about nasty socialites who are calculating in their cruelty toward one another. The 1939 film starred Rosalind Russell as the nosy friend, Joan Crawford as the one to steal a husband, and Norma Shearer as the innocent wife who loses her husband. The 2008 version involves an updated story, and features an array of actresses, including Bette Midler as a talent agent, Jada Pinkett Smith as a gay woman, Eva Mendes as an opportunist, Meg Ryan as the victim, Candice Bergen as her sly mother, and Annette Bening as the slippery friend. The story itself is evergreen when it comes to trust and the reality of our women friends.

Styles of Frenemies

While I was interviewing women for this chapter, the types of frenemies became apparent, with their behavior frequently manifesting in "stealing" another woman's partner or husband, or purposely interfering with a woman's reputation at work or in the community. This kind of "thieving" exhibits the destructive face of friendship. As Dr. Donald Cohen explains it, these behaviors are the result of being desperate. "Narcissism takes over when a woman is lonely or unhappy in her own life," he explains, "and she thinks only of herself. The jealousy and competition follow and fidelity is forgotten."

The Deficient One

Another possibility is that the frenemy develops over time; at first she is your friend and she is drawn to you although she feels she is less than you. Although you know she's the jealous sort, you don't see it directed at you. In Tom Perrotta's novel *The Abstinence Teacher,* Trisha, a minor character in the book, describes her best friend, Eve, with whom she's been friends since kindergarten. Initially it was Trisha who was perceived as "'the smart one, the athletic one, and later, the pretty one.' Eve was the admirer, it was her job to stand loyally by Trisha's side," writes Perrotta. In high school, Trisha was infuriated when she realized that Eve had surpassed her. Meanwhile, Eve did not know her own power. Finally, when Eve became engaged, Trisha's idolspizing came to a crescendo, and one evening she seduced Eve's fiancé, Thad, while Eve was asleep upstairs.

The Blatant Taker

This friend takes advantage openly, and at first you might be shocked, but it's confusing because you like her, and everyone needs friends. Or you are the sitting duck: You've just broken up with a boyfriend, or your sister just moved out of town, or your mother is sick, or you miscarried . . . you *want* a friend, and here she is. Often she is a leader or a sacrificer, since both of these types of friends can be inviting, and it confuses the issue. Since you have given her your trust, it can take a while before it sinks in that she is in it for herself. Interestingly enough, when a woman recognizes this, these relationships can still succeed. For instance, Gabby, 46, who lives in Florida, where she volunteers her time, believes that although she used a friend for social connections and became entangled with the woman's husband, the friendship works.

I met this friend, Lillie, when I wanted to know the right people. Then I had an affair with her husband, whom I found attractive. I think I did it because Lillie seemed to have everything. So I sneaked around with her husband for a year to see how it would be. I have no regrets, but I know it was wrong. I suppose the friendship with her was false, but the affair is over and I still get invited to her charity events. Whether she knows or not, we're still friends. We mix with the same crowd and neither of us is going to give that up, so we both play by the rules, meaning we move on and there are no hard feelings. No one wants to dig very deep around here, and that's fine with me. I know some people would find me callous, but I'm okay with what I did, and no one is the worse for wear. It's all a game.

The Persuasive Diplomat

It would be difficult to pull off the conduct described above without being convincing—downright disarming—as a friend. Persuasion is a tool in our society, and women use it well. When a friend has polished the technique and combines it with reason, it is irresistible for the innocent bystander. Women who are deceived by a frenemy frequently express respect for her thoughts and remain awed and captivated by her energy. They find her magnetizing, interesting, and fun; part trophy friend, part leader, the persuasive idolspizer is difficult to give up. Jan, 56, who lives in Maryland, where she works as a physical therapist, was not initially aware of her friend's real intentions.

People would want to befriend me because I'm married to a local sports figure and they could get free tickets and invitations to parties and meet people. I have one friend who was always there for me and upbeat compared to most women I know—she was fun to be with and could get me to go anywhere, anytime. She would talk me into things, and when I look back, it all had to do with getting her somewhere, but I did it. Then things got tighter and I couldn't invite her to all the events. She complained about me and she even turned on me when she learned who was still invited—making up stories that weren't true. I walked away from the friendship, but I kept thinking it was a loss. I didn't want to be without her and I made these ridiculous efforts to hold it together. I've always been like that, the one desperate for friends.

The Wolf in Sheep's Clothing

Surely the frenemy is a slap in the face to all that we have idealized about our women friends, and yet women repeatedly seem surprised by the trajectory of these relationships. In an essay that ran in *The New York Times* on February 7, 2008, "It's Not the Job I Despise, It's You," Lisa Belkin illustrated two female colleagues who "even joined forces when the work piled up" and shared lunches, until there was a problem over vacation time. Belkin quoted one of the injured parties, who described her estranged colleague as leaving "her trash from lunch in my trash can, smelly things like blue cheese or cauliflower or tuna." Can it be that the expectations are just too high in these friendships or the fallout too steep, resulting in sinister behavior?

Toughening Up

A study by Lois Verbrugge, "Multiplexity in Adult Friendships," addresses how women select friends based on commonality

and networking, since an "overlap of roles, exchanges or affili-
ations" affects social relationships. If we apply this concept to
the two female coworkers/close friends who become frenemies, in Belkin's article, what Verbrugge details as the factors
of multiplexity makes sense. Women meet at work or through
mutual friends or family and are "more (or less) attracted to
each other and make greater (or lesser) efforts to get together,"
she writes. In this way, multiplexity offers contact and prefer-
ences, and the result is that some women become friends
while others do not. However, it is the unraveling of these se-
lected friendships based on an initial attraction that can be
complicated. If the friend is a user or a trophy friend, she has
the easiest exit route and the toughest skin; a leader (who can
be a user too) also has the ability to let it roll off her back.
Those who suffer most at the hands of a frenemy or an idolspizing friend are doormats, sacrificers, and, to a lesser degree,
mirroring friends.

Consider Lisee, 37, who works in a pharmacy and has two
daughters. She lives in Massachusetts.

My friend doesn't care if I'm a single mother or having financial
problems while she's married and has a comfortable life. She only
cares about what I have that she wanted—it's the prestige for her,
and she wants it all. So she has come to dislike me, or she thinks
that I won this round. I can feel her anger and how she's changed
toward me. She's not really my friend anymore; she's someone
who says she's my friend. Mostly I'm disappointed and waiting for
it to get better, for her to be kinder somehow.

The User + Jealousy = the Frenemy

There isn't only a user mentality in the woman who idolspizes but a simmering rage that somehow her friend is more fortunate or has what she wants. What happens in these incidents is that the self-serving aspect of the friend deteriorates into something bleaker, and the frenemy is born. The idea of the tormentor and her tormented is exhibited in Margaret Atwood's novel *Cat's Eye*. While the narrator, Elaine Risley, recalls her long-ago school days, when she filled the role of the sacrificer, continually mistreated by the nasty leader of her group, Cordelia, whom she both admired and abhorred, this novel is also a tale of just deserts. Cordelia does not finish high school, while Elaine goes on to graduate college and become a famous artist. Yet she is scarred and haunted by her past, though she is the strong one and Cordelia is now in an institution, having attempted suicide.

Contrary to Elaine Risley, who forges her own path away from her frenemy, are those women who do *not* leave once the writing is on the wall. Much of a woman's decision in conjunction with the frenemy depends on her own defenses in entering, enduring, exiting, or remaining.

Self-Esteem and the Frenemy

The frenemy is devoid of self-esteem and punishes her friends by taking what isn't rightfully hers or by wishing her friends ill. Over 60 percent of my interviewees felt that their mothers taught them how to interact with their female friends, both positively and negatively.

If a lack of self-esteem contributes to the frenemy mentality, Aimee Lee Ball's article "The New and Improved Self-
Esteem," which appeared in *O, The Oprah Magazine* in January
2008, investigates a new take on the concept. Ball reported
that research by psychologists Carol Dweck and Roy Baumeis-
ter indicates that contrary to popular thought, endless, unconditional praise for our children isn't helpful, while "self-control,
self-regulation . . . effort, strategy, perseverance" are the keys
to building the right kind of self-esteem. If this more measured, less over-the-top form, doused with a sense of reality,
can help future generations of young women, there might be
less need to undermine a friend because you resent her good
fortune. For example, Glory, 46, who lives in New England
and is a single mother of two, realized who her friends were
after her divorce.

When I first got divorced and thought I'd get a job, my closest friends were behind me. Then while I was hunting for work,
having been a stay-at-home mom, my divorce settlement
came through and I didn't need a job. That's when my closest
friends weren't happy for me. Some of them distanced themselves, and at first I thought it was my fault; I thought I'd done
something wrong. But I hadn't, and it was my belief in myself
that got me through such a tough time—a husband dumping me,
then friends leaving me because I wouldn't be a poor divorcée. I
kept thinking they'd be happy for me, and say, Lucky you, but it
was nothing of the sort. I think they wanted me to be poor and
single.

When I was growing up, no one in my family ever said I was
great, but I always did well in school and I had a scholarship to college. When the chips were down, I knew I could fall back on myself.

That's why I filed away the true friends and let the others go, and that's why I never felt down and out, like some women do during such a bad time—I had faith in myself.

Glory's self-esteem is not a reflection of a doting mother, but a strong sense of self, which she utilized as a tool during a trying period in her life. Rather than a victim of a false sense of self-esteem, making her a more likely target for the frenemy, Glory was able to discern real female friendship. She was not lured into unpleasant scenarios, such as those described earlier in this chapter by Alice and Jane, both of whom are doormats with sacrificer tendencies.

Obligatory Friendships

There is the possibility that our attraction to some of our friends overshadows our instincts, and a false sense of trust ensues. Such a trajectory is characterized in Collette DeDonato's article "An Open and Shut Marriage," which ran in *The New York Times* on February 3, 2008. DeDonato wrote how several years after she was married, her "good friend" confessed to a crush on her husband. "I didn't feel particularly threatened by this friend. I trusted her," DeDonato recounted. However, once her husband and this friend spent time together openly, DeDonato realized she couldn't subscribe to an open marriage. While she and her husband worked it out, the friendship did not survive. DcDonato explained, "As one might imagine, the good friend and I did not remain good friends. The bond was the weaker one, it turned out."

Gabby, who earlier in this chapter documented a yearlong affair with her friend Lillie's husband, is an example of a friend to whom you feel you owe nothing. Although it's not clear that Lillie learned about the affair, there are women who cling to a frenemy after a discovery of betrayal, for social or work reasons. As Dr. Ronnie Burak points out, women who stick with friends in unproductive friendships are fearful of being alone, which is a recurring theme. "These women figure it's better to have a lousy friend than no friend at all, but these insecurities are on a developmental scale, and it's for that reason that the women settle." The question becomes why one stays in a relationship that is clearly the most negative of all, worse than a compromising friendship with a user, who frequently has some redeeming qualities.

Cutting Loose?

As I wrote this chapter, the mind-set of a woman who idolspizes her friend became apparent, as did the actions such a woman will take in the name of friendship. We have observed that there is little guilt involved with the frenemy's actions, and for some time, she is usually able to deceive her innocent friend. As expert opinion bears out, narcissism has a role in the frenemy's attitude, as does an underlying personal discontent. Sixty percent of my interviewees confessed to having used or idolspized another woman and to being competitive and/or jealous, while staying friends.

It appears that the frenemy is rarely the one to instigate the end of these friendships. Of those who are the object of the frenemy's "affection," or idolspized, 40 percent wanted to stay connected to the perpetrator, regardless of the treatment they'd received. If we break it down further, once the innocent friend becomes wise to what kind of damage the frenemy is capable of, 35 percent leave the relationship, and 35 percent stay. Fifteen percent of frenemies are able to maintain their pseudo-friendship somehow, and only 15 percent of frenemies decide to leave their friends.

Giving Her Up

What do you do when there is no return on the investment?
Once the friend's actions are clear, it is time to move on, overcoming your concern about losing friends or social position. That being said, we have witnessed the extreme measures one woman will take toward another in the guise of friendship.

What do you do when the friend is actually harming you or someone close to you?
When there is nothing but negativity, using, and rivalry surrounding the friendship, women will take charge and call it quits. Usually, there has to be a cataclysmic event surrounding the breakup.

Sorting It Out

What of our friend who "turns the table"—the friend we cannot really trust?
When women try to leave, they tend to recall the excitement and happy aspects of the frenemy and determine to make it work, factoring in all that they know about this friend.

Have you yourself been a frenemy or idolspized?

Another rationale is that the victim of a frenemy has a history of having been one to someone else and now the balance has changed. In this way, she's more likely to work it out with her own idolspizing friend.

SEVEN

The Trophy Friend: Conquest in Motion

✗ Does your friend seek out women she can win over?

✗ Is she always conscious of how her friends live and what they have?

✗ Does she leave a friend once she has accomplished her seduction?

✗ Are you sucked into her MO?

✗ Do you lose yourself in the friendship?

✗ Are your standards murky—do you give too much to get too little?

Affirmative answers tell us you have a trophy friend.

"I met this woman a few years ago at a spa and she totally manipulated me into being her friend," recalled Carolina, 43, who designs children's clothes, and lives in Connecticut. "It lasted for six months before a red flag went up. From the start, it was stupid me. She looked like a Victoria's Secret model. She spent tons of money and time on her fake boobs, on her hair, at the gym. She was so different from anyone I'd ever met, and at first we went on shopping sprees together, and out to lunch. I didn't know she had this secret life, where all these men were taking care of her, giving her money. She befriended me when she was looking for a place to stay and knew that my boyfriend and I had a nice home. I was so open, so willing to invite her in. I thought a friend like this would make my life more glamorous.

"She had me wrapped around her dirty little finger once I made her comfortable in the guest bedroom. I think I fell for her and the idea that we could be friends because she was spontaneous and fun. She treated me the way she treated the men she picked up, like they were special. I was such a victim, and she was a pro. I realized that when I learned she was sleeping with my boyfriend, then I figured she'd done it with other women too; she'd gone after them to get what she wanted—and won at it."

The **trophy friend** is out for the conquest of making you her friend. To this end, you elevate her to a new level and she, in turn, offers you something you don't already have. This friend is capable of seduction; she discovers you, and it is thrilling to be together, connected to the exclusion of the outside world. It is very enticing to be wooed; women describe the sensation as feeling like romantic love, in that the initial stages are exhilarating. If we apply Robert J. Sternberg's love triangle paradigm, mentioned in Chapter 3, the components are intimacy, passion, and commitment. While we have witnessed all three of these qualities in a variety of friends, including the doormat, the sacrificer, the sharer, the mirroring friend (more to follow in Chapter 8), and the authentic friend (more on this in Chapter 10), the trophy friend is savvy about intimacy and passion but falls short on commitment. Several interviewees said they only realized this when the friendship was no longer new and they began to question what was going on.

In the film *Notes on a Scandal,* Cate Blanchett's character, Sheba Hart, is initially seduced by Judi Dench's character, Barbara Covett, a bitter woman who has entrapped younger women before. Sheba is naive about Barbara's plan to consume her and unaware that she is a feather in this woman's cap. At first Sheba considers it a good thing to have a new friend at her new job—a real advantage. Soon enough Barbara breaks Sheba's trust and reveals that Sheba is involved with a 15-year-old student. This bleak tale reminds us of the risk one takes in opening up to another person and how once female friendship sours, women are able to harm each other. As psychologist Barton Goldsmith explains it, "Seldom is it a real friendship when someone has an agenda. Then the friendship represents power and the seduction is part of the power play." Even for those women who are aware of how a friendship with a trophy friend plays out, the temptation can be hard to resist.

Mold Beyond Motive

In the twenty-first century, the trophy friend represents connections of all sorts: financial, social, and professional. According to research conducted by Veniegas and Peplau, there are dominance patterns in friendships despite the fact that we want there to be parity and mutual respect. In their study "Power and the Quality of Same Sex Friendships" the researchers note that "social power is commonly defined as one person's ability to influence another."

More than half the women with whom I spoke for this chapter admitted that they knew it wasn't easy or comfortable to be caught in the web of the trophy friend. The vicissitudes of such relationships play out as follows.

Repeat Patterns

Women dread alienating this type of friend, and once tantalized, they remain vulnerable. A woman will meet a trophy friend and the relationship will take its course; if the friendship comes to an end, a trophy friend may appear in her life again.

Roxie, 41, a hospital administrator and single mother, lives in Maryland.

At times this friend and I are in synch. Years ago we dated the same guys and sort of passed them around. It's hard to believe it was okay, but we managed. We got over that stage and both of us got married and had children. The next stage was that whatever she recommended I do for my girls, I did. I was sort of a sponge for her ideas and recommendations. Now we're older and the kids are older and I'm still impressed with her, that she's so accomplished, and I'm still in awe of her and happy that she's my friend. When we get together, I feel judged by her, as if I have to please her and do what she wants. I'm not sure what I do for her, since someone's always got to offer something for her to be there. Maybe it's my career and happy love life—maybe I'm the one on her shelf who has that. I try not to be sucked into thinking she's better than I am or to get caught up in what she wants out of the friendship. The truth is, I'm happier to be with her than without her. And it works for me, too, to have this friend who is so well known.

Beguiling Acts

How can one resist the friend who is disarming, who has to have us? What is missing here is an equal playing field. The charisma of the trophy friend is often too strong for the friend to fight for her rights in the relationship.

Patti, 50, a social worker, is married with three children and lives in a Northeastern suburb.

All these years I wanted to be so close to my friend from high school who was the most popular girl. She was so much fun and so crazy when we were young that the times we lost touch have always bothered me. No matter what she did, and she wasn't a good friend for sure, I was hoping to be close friends. I would go out of my way to be with her, and yet she always had her group of friends who were more important to her than I was. The past few years I've been asking myself what's good about this friendship, when every time I see her I feel happy and depressed at once. It's always on her terms. Finally I decided that there's nothing special or good or kind about her and I'm letting go. I've had enough.

Blinders On

A woman will meet this friend and be seduced by her, only to learn that it was a ploy, that she's been used on some level (trophy friends do mix with users). Oftentimes the trophy friend is out to broaden her social circle or to meet someone important. Usually the innocent friend wants to remain friends, and cannot quite fathom why the trophy friend is the way she is.

Layla, 37, who is a teacher, was recently married and lives in a Midwestern city.

This is the friend who makes everyone else seem less important. I'll cancel plans to be with her. I know she isn't even nice, but I can't help caring so much about hearing from her. Since she knows this, she is demanding and bossy and I basically do whatever she wants. She has manipulated situations in the past so that she's invited places that I'm not and I just wait and hope that at the last minute, I will be included too. She's the one who found me, at work, when she first got to the job and knew no one. Now everyone is her best friend and I'm sort of fading away. If she's your friend, people think more of you and she knows this—we're all at her mercy.

Girl Crushes

While a "girl crush," according to Stephanie Rosenbloom in her August 11, 2005, piece in *The New York Times*, "She's So Cool, So Smart, So Beautiful: Must Be a Girl Crush," is not a new phenomenon, young women are able to discuss their feelings more today than in the past. Dr. Helen Fisher a biological anthropologist whom Rosenbloom quoted, describes young women as able to fall in love with other young women "without feeling sexual toward them, without the intention to marry them."

Daniella, who is 21, is a full-time student, and lives in Southern California, has had a "crush" on one friend for the past four years.

My friend and I were in high school together but didn't get friendly until our last year. She is everything I'd like to be: tall and thin and beautiful, with fabulous clothes. I really look forward to being with her, and it's more exciting than being with my other friends. But I also know that she can manipulate things: with the guys, with our plans to go out at night. I see that she does it but I still have this feeling for her.

The Pecking Order

In the feature film *Clueless,* based on the 1816 novel *Emma,* by Jane Austen, Alicia Silverstone plays Cher, the leader and a trophy friend, and Stacey Dash plays her best friend, Dionne. Although both girls are popular, Dionne is second fiddle to Cher, who is so inviting and lively, she's hard to resist. It's fortunate that Cher also has real feelings, despite being spoiled and self-indulgent. This theme is also found in television twosomes of the past fifty years who are trophy friends with some heart. The television series *I Love Lucy,* which first aired in 1951, starred Lucille Ball as Lucy. Her sidekick was Ethel, her neighbor, played by Vivian Vance. Lucy was surely seductive in her crazy schemes and constant pleas to Ethel to get on board. While Lucy needed Ethel as her primary audience, it was Lucy's outrageous acts that spiced up Ethel's life.

It was a similarly stratified friendship for the women in the television series *The Honeymooners,* which aired for only one season, in 1955. Audrey Meadows played Alice, the wife of Jackie Gleason's character, Ralph Kramden, and Joyce Randolph played Trixie, the wife of Art Carney's character, Ed Norton. In this case, the men are the schemers, especially Ralph, and the women the skeptics. Again, however, Alice is a trophy friend/leader, who encourages Trixie to take a stand against the get-rich-quick plans of their husbands, and to be her cohort. In the sixties, the cartoon series *The Flintstones*, a satire of modern life that took place in the Stone Age, had two female best friends, Wilma, the wife of Fred Flintstone, and Betty, the wife of Fred's best friend, Barney Rubble. The same formula applies; Wilma was the trophy friend/leader and could convince Betty to follow. When she gave birth to her daughter, Pebbles, it was enticing enough for Betty to adopt Bamm-Bamm, an orphaned boy.

Ripe for the Seduction

In each of these instances, we recognize the argument for and the argument against an involvement with a trophy friend, one who unquestionably has the ability to sway her friends, and whose powers are apparent. Consider Annemarie, a 47-year-old accountant who lives in Boston, who struggles to let go of this kind of friend.

I have a lot of guilt about the kind of friend I'm supposed to be. I cancel plans more often than I keep them, but then this one friend calls and I'm mush. She tells me her problems—and she always has problems—and I'm a good listener, but mostly I feel I want to be there for her; I want to please her. I sit on the phone for hours if that's what she needs. I'll blow off almost anyone for her. I can't say no. But I'm not really doing anything right; probably, I'm doing things wrong. It's always been our dynamic. I've been through so much: a bad divorce, a troubled child, a sick parent. I can't lean on this friend, she's not willing to give much to me, and then I start to doubt myself. Then I'm the best friend to her, although she's not the kind of friend I can count on. I can't even explain this. It's like I have to be with her; I have to have this friend. I'd feel terrible if she wasn't in my life, and I can't even explain why. It isn't healthy; it keeps me from healthier friends since no one has time these days for everyone. The time I give to her is the time I don't give to a better, more dependable friend.

Annemarie is a doormat, while her trophy friend is part user. That Annemarie *knows* this and cannot resist her friend raises questions about her self-confidence. Women who are intrigued by the trophy friend are not always anchored in their own lives, nor do they have enough self-respect to be grounded. The perception of unequal strength fosters an unhealthy balance in these relationships.

Lies We Tell Ourselves

In my book about why women lie, *Little White Lies, Deep Dark Secrets*, I was struck by how women lie to themselves when it comes to relationships, including our love relationships and in our roles as mothers, daughters, sisters, and friends. Women lie about their feelings of friendship because sometimes it is just easier than facing who this friend is and isn't, and to what degree her needs are getting met. When the longing for the friendship to succeed is strong, women tend to dig in despite the inherent problems. According to Dr. Ronnie Burak, the attraction to the trophy friend may be about one's childhood. "If you didn't get your fair share when you were growing up, this is reflected in who you choose as friends. What attracts you is what was missing in some way, even if it ends up not working in your favor."

Although trust is an issue in any friendship, when it

comes to the trophy friend, the one who is seduced finds the magnetism overwhelming. The face-to-face quality of female friendships makes it difficult to pull away as the trophy friend's intentions become apparent. No wonder women deceive themselves that the friendship is more rewarding than it is.

While Carolina's experience is one that reminds us of how careful we need to be when encountering new friends, does this mean we have to be suspicious? At the outset of the notorious friendship between Linda Tripp and Monica Lewinsky, Tripp sought out Lewinsky, according to Damian Whitworth's Times Online column "Oral History: The Monica Lewinsky Scandal Ten Years On," which ran on January 15, 2008. Whitworth wrote that Linda Tripp "befriended Lewinsky, who had been moved out of the White House by aides concerned about her relationship with the President. Tripp became the younger woman's confidante as she agonized about what Clinton really thought of her." Whitworth also pointed out that "it became clear that she [Tripp] was also out to get Clinton and manipulated the situation. . . . She led Lewinsky on to discuss Clinton while she was taping, she encouraged her to use a courier service to send her packages so that there would be a paper trail and she insisted that Lewinsky hold on to the famous blue Gap dress."

Enticed by Our Friends

Women interviewed for this chapter spoke of the unknown aspect of friendship, of opening yourself up only to discover that it is not safe. Over 30 percent of those who had encountered a trophy friend believed this could happen again, and they have their guard up. For instance, Rae, 50, who works at a newspaper and lives in Pennsylvania, fell for a friend whose sincerity and intentions became questionable.

Eight years ago, we moved to a new town where I knew no one. I joined the gym and the parents' association and tried to meet women through my children. The one woman I felt could be my friend turned out to be my worst nightmare. She was a journalist also and we seemed to have a lot in common. Her boys were the same ages as my boys and she loved sports, the way I do. We were both athletic, working mothers. She had first met me with my husband at the kids' school, and it was afterward that she made this beeline for me. She invited us all to her house for dinner and made all these grand gestures to be my friend, carpooling, inviting my boys over after school, going to lunch with me. I was happy since no one else seemed very friendly.

We went out to dinner as couples a few times, but mostly she would drive over to the house on weekends and visit with her kids. It was all very casual, and it took me a while to realize that she was so nice to me because she wanted my husband. Later I learned they were having an affair. I was doubly betrayed, by him and by her. I remember I used to say to him, before I knew the truth, that this friend made it easier to have moved to where we were living; that's how duped I was. Today I wouldn't make a new friend without doing a background check of some kind.

Age and life experience are meant to render us wiser and more discerning when it comes to our friendships, yet women of every age spoke with me about the perils of the trophy friend. Joan Borysenko notes in her book *A Woman's Book of Life* that she believes "the very soul of the feminine worldview" is how interdependent women are, and "that relationship provides a context in which all participants can grow and become empowered, the emergent whole evolving into more than the sum of its parts." Yet when women feel they were fooled, not much of this concept holds water. In this way, the interdependence of women can go awry, and we are let down or worse, taken advantage of and hurt in the process.

Belly of the Beast

There are friends who both caution and titillate us. A frightening tale is told in the film *Single White Female*, a psychological thriller starring Jennifer Jason Leigh as Hedra Carlson and Bridget Fonda as Allison Jones. When Hedra moves in to Allison's apartment as a roommate, she befriends Allison and feeds her ego so that Allison is unwittingly seduced. But when Hedy starts to imitate Allison (bordering on identity theft), Allison becomes dubious, and too late she realizes she has been roped in and that people's lives are in danger.

For women who are connected by a man, and can never be friends themselves because they are too similar, there is the film *The Grifters,* starring Anjelica Huston as Lilly, Annette Bening as Myra, and John Cusack as Roy. Roy is Lilly's son and Myra's boyfriend; all three characters are con artists. The women are trophy friends by nature, who are trying to beat each other at the con. It ends badly and reminds us that while a lack of trust is inevitable in this world, things might have gone much better if the women had worked together. In everyday life, the stakes are not as high, obviously, but the trophy friend can wreak havoc. For example, Georgia, 38, who lives in Detroit, where she works as a freelance publicist, had to sever a friendship that she once valued.

I had this friend who was wearing me out, and she was my neighbor, so it was hard to avoid her. She had a young, crack-addicted boyfriend and she kept demanding more of me as things got worse with the boyfriend. I think I was hooked on her for a while because she was so attractive and chic, so hip and fun. It's always good to have a friend like that, one who knows where to go and what's in. I needed that since my life is pretty boring. That was what did it for me, that she knew a world I didn't know. It seemed like fun but it wasn't after a while. I guess her life was too much a mess, and what she did by becoming my friend was get me involved in all her crap so I could console her. It got so that when she would knock on my door, I dove to the floor and wouldn't answer. She'd go on and on, asking me what I thought, and it was my fault for being involved in the first place.

Loneliness and Seduction

Most women find that the idea of being disenfranchised can be an upsetting thought. Whether a woman is 21, 41, or 61, and breaks up with her boyfriend, moves to a new town, or loses touch with old friends, a sense of loneliness frequently descends. Women say this makes them more vulnerable to a trophy friend, someone who appears to be socially connected and has enough agency to attract others. As Allison, 24, who is a graduate student living in Michigan, described it, feeling alone makes one hungry for companionship.

I moved here to go to grad school, but everyone is so unfriendly, and I don't know a soul. I look around and see that everyone else's

life is in order, and I feel like time is passing me by. I don't have anyone to date, and I decided to save money by not living in the dorms,
so I found this crummy apartment off campus. It's weird and quiet
on my street though I live in a college town. I was losing confidence,
and that's why I became friends with this woman who is untrust-
worthy. She made noise about introducing me to people and about
how we'd do things together, but she always cancels and doesn't
mean a thing she says. I fell for her because I'm desperate for a
friend and I thought she'd be the one who organized us and got me
to parties. She definitely is that type—outgoing, social. She's a winner, and having her as a friend would help. I think she thought I was
attractive enough to take with her. So it would have worked out
fine. I just wonder why she bothered with me at all if she didn't
mean it.

The Mean-Spirited Friend

There is another ingredient in these relationships as well, and
that is a streak of meanness. While this can apply to any kind of
friendship, to varying degrees, if the trophy friend is mean-
spirited, this is rarely discovered during the initial meetings. As
Richard A. Friedman, M.D., wrote in his article in *The New
York Times* on February 6, 2007, "About That Mean Streak of
Yours: Psychiatry Can Do Only So Much," "human meanness
is far more common than all the mental illness in the population combined." Friedman described this condition as an "es-
sential human trait." Still, we know it is not appreciated and is
definitely a negative in any friendship. For Dolores, 62, who
runs her own business and lives in New England, her long-
standing friendship with a woman she describes as "very inviting" ended when Dolores hit her threshold.

This woman and I were friends for years and we spent hours on the phone some nights, sharing our thoughts and our lives. We'd met through mutual friends, and she definitely wanted to be my friend since I'm the go-to person, in my own way. I think she saw me as well connected in our town and she wanted to branch out. I tried to introduce her to my friends, but no one liked her and everyone called her mean and superficial. When she was widowed, I was very supportive and fixed her up with a few single men I know. None of this worked out, so we became phone pals, lunch pals, and shopping pals. She and I both love clothes, and that was enough for a while.

But she was jealous of me, and she always made these comments about how I don't look as young as people say I do and that I'm not as hardworking as I could be. I'd given her some business through my business, and this wasn't fair. I had to reexamine what was happening. She'd come to me, she had asked that we be introduced, she had sought me out and wanted my friendship, and I fell for it. The truth is, she's just plain mean and nasty, and the jealousy comes after that. I guess I've had enough and I have backed off. Whatever made her so great in the beginning is long gone.

Trophy + Trophy = Satisfying Friendship

The mixed message of the trophy friend is that she is not simply someone to avoid at all costs, but someone to prize as well; she can be graceful, popular, lively, smart, well connected, and friendly. There are times and occasions where a mutual need can satisfy both parties and the friendship can be a success. We see this in the film version of Fannie Flagg's novel *Fried Green Tomatoes at the Whistlestop Café*, in which Evelyn Couch, played by Kathy Bates, gravitates toward an elderly woman,

Ninny Threadgoode, played by Jessica Tandy, who lives at a nursing home. As Ninny regales Evelyn with her family saga from the 1920s, the women grow closer based on both parties' attachment to this oral history. This kind of friendship occurred for Janie, 52, an attorney who lives in Vermont, and claims she was *not* in search of a friend when she became "entranced" with someone she met at a seminar.

I have sisters and daughters and I don't need any more friends. I'm not that social, and I enjoy being with family on weekends, especially since I work long hours during the week. I don't have much time in my life, so for me to be so taken with someone is unusual. I met an older woman who began to tell me about her life in Europe during World War II, what happened to her family, and how she began life here afterward. Her story was so far from my life that I was really interested and caught up in it. We began to meet for coffee and I would ask her all these questions.

I doubt we'd be friends if she hadn't shared what happened with me; I doubt I would have cared much to speak with her. Now she is truly a friend, and I'm the one who seeks her out—she has more friends and a far busier and broader life than I do. I find her story fascinating, and it makes me appreciate my life and its lack of drama. She also asks me about my world, but let's face it, it's pretty ordinary compared to what she's lived through. I tell her anyway, about my job, my kids, my ex-husband, and she listens and sometimes offers advice.

The Ways We Are Seduced

The cause and the effect of the trophy friend are entwined, and the crossover of the mirroring friend, the doormat, and the user often resonates in these unions. In the twenty-first century, the five most common trophy friend scenarios involve the following:

Money and Friends. In our capitalistic society, it stands to reason that we might fall for someone who has deep pockets, as if in some magical way, it will benefit us. This might not be logical, but it is an age-old scenario for women choosing men and vice versa, and a method for women friends finding each other. The trophy friend is well aware that money is always compelling. Consider Elizabeth, 48, who does volunteer work and lives in a Southern city. Part user, she purposely seeks out trophy friends for the return on her investment.

Now that I'm older, I don't waste time on friends who don't live like I do. The one friend who is new in my life is both glamorous and wealthy. I wanted to be with her because of who she knows and the kind of life she leads. I can attract friends because of my wealth, and it's fine to admit that. Why not? I'm attracted to these friends for the same reason; it works both ways.

Social Connections. "Who knows who" has been an important aspect of friendship for women for centuries. The trophy friend is found in circles that revolve around sports, lifestyle, and the social register. If the trophy friend has social power, she is often a leader as well. For example, Ruth, 37, who works in a family business, senses that people want to be seduced by her and that she evokes idolspizing.

Sure, people have always been pulled in by our family name. I'm never sure why someone wants to be with me; I always think they're intrigued by my background and who I know. I'm not that friendly, but that's because I feel like I don't have to be—everyone is friendly to me and hopes they'll get close. And I know that no one's a true friend. So I just reel friends in, if I want, and sometimes I'm happier than other times with how it works out.

Children. In a period when great emphasis is placed on motherhood and the division between stay-at-home mothers and working mothers continues, a trophy friend among mothers conjures a sense of dread and opportunity. The mother who wields influence is both a leader and a trophy friend, one who carefully plucks the other mothers. In this competitive atmosphere, women describe being used and being users themselves. For example, Daryll, 35, who lives in a suburb in New Jersey, is a stay-at-home mother. Part leader/part user/part trophy friend, she prides herself on being a class mother for each of her four children's grades.

I feel the mothers buzzing around me, and I like it. I devote myself to this so I'm not the one wanting to be invited in but instead can do the inviting. So now the mothers are trying to be my best friend, and I let them think they are, when it's not the case. I'm sought after, while if I hadn't taken on this role, I'd be begging for these women to include me and getting rope burns myself. For each child, I'm the mother of note, so to speak. It is time-consuming but worth every minute.

The Workplace. To get ahead, meet people, and change companies, the trophy friend is always looking to network and expand; friends represent new opportunities. Women describe meetings where they size one another up, willing to be reeled in, almost afraid to resist the seduction. Consider Adele, 44, who works at a corporation and lives in a large city.

> There are some women I won't work with—I know better. I watch everyone else fall for them, thinking how fabulous these bosses are. But they're not, and I don't catch the fever; I don't start feeling like I'm missing something if I'm not on their team. Then I end up leaving one office and going to another and it seems like the same person is there—she's cool and confident and the others have to be with her. That woman always has the best job and is such a fake.

Love Fest. When *The New York Times* ran an article on April 13, 2008, by Stephanie Rosenbloom, "For Housewives, She's the Hot Ticket," about Jackie Warner, Warner was described as "the lesbian fitness trainer" who believes that her "top demographic" consists of housewives. According to the article, straight, married women are fascinated by Warner and enroll in her classes. There are women who are part doormat/part sacrificer who find trophy friends very appealing. Sally, 56, who lives in rural Massachusetts, explained how she is infatuated with one of her female friends.

> I'm not a lesbian, but I had this friend and we were in love without sex. She had to be with me and I liked that, and I had to be with her. We also shared interests but she was more accomplished. When we had a falling-out, I was devastated; it really was like losing a boyfriend, I was so taken with her. This was unexpected, and I've had to recover. The friendship was too intense and I was too easy.

Arm Candy. If a mother was a trophy friend herself or was intrigued by her trophy friends, it influences the daughter.

Nadia, 34, who works as an accountant and lives in Georgia, described her mother as a social butterfly who put her friends ahead of her children.

My mother has always been so taken with her friends that she worried about their needs more than she worried about her three daughters when we were little. I saw how caught up she was with the social scene and how easily she moved with the crowd, never having a thought of her own. She was always worried about being left out, too, as if these women weren't her real friends, but she wanted them to be. This taught me to care less about my girlfriends and to worry more about my marriage and my son. I don't want to be so into a scene that I can't think for myself or that I worry about being forgotten or no longer the flavor du jour. It seemed like a waste of energy for my mom, who is a smart woman. Maybe it's because she didn't work that it mattered so much, and now that she's older, she still cares, still wants to be an adornment. I decided to work partly so I wouldn't be stuck at home, thinking about whether I'd be included in the next girls' night out.

Shades of Seduction

While Nadia's mother was influenced by her friends, it also seems she was a doormat in her crowd, which contributed to her ability to be seduced. Thus much of our behavior when it comes to friendship is environmental as well as genetic or biological. But we also fall into a category by our personal style: One woman is more giving than her friend, another is more reticent or more of a leader, another is a trophy friend. In any of these cases, there is the intimacy factor. "People jump into intimacy before they can trust the person. This definitely happens in women's friendships, and it's a big mistake. Then people are disappointed and hurt," Dr. Claire Owen remarks.

At some point, women report, a more honest approach to those friends who have not served them well kicks in. This stands to reason, although the trophy friend can be irresistible and intoxicating. Therefore, it is a bold step to "clean your closet," preserving the friendships that are healthy and letting go of those that are not.

When to Ditch the Trophy Friend

Is this friend draining you?

When your interactions with the friend are affecting other parts of your life, it's time to reconsider the friendship. Fifty percent of the women interviewed for this chapter felt that the trophy friend was destructive, and in the end, they made a clean break.

Are you losing your core values in the relationship?

It is one thing to view the friendship as a way to "win," but if you have lost faith or no longer respect yourself, it is not a healthy situation.

Have you found that the advantages you imagined with a trophy friend are not that important?

If your trophy friend represents an advantage socially or at work, but beyond that doesn't interest you at all, it is time to move away from the user aspect of this and seek friends whom you care about.

When to Tough It Out

Does the balance works for both parties?
If you have a scheme in mind and it blends in with your trophy friendship, it can suffice. Fifty percent of the women in this chapter reported that they hang in *as* a trophy friend or *for* a trophy friend, while recognizing the challenges.

Can you be honest with this friend and get beyond the seductive aspects of the friendship?
If you are hooked by a trophy friend initially and then fall into a healthy rapport with her despite the initial premise, this can be a manageable friendship.

Are you comfortable with yourself in the relationship?
Over half of my interviewees sincerely wanted the trophy friend to be their friend and felt good about the relationship. When positive qualities emerge in the friendships, it can be rewarding.

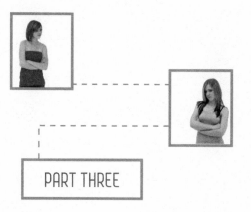

PART THREE

Those We Keep:
The Evolution of the Female Friend

EIGHT

The Mirroring Friend: Circumstantial Bonds

✗ Do you and your friend reflect each other in every facet of your life?

✗ Do friends and family who are outside your experience seem distant?

✗ Do you feel you speak the same language as your closest friend?

✗ Does it feel safe to be with a friend who is so similar?

✗ Are you exclusive with your friend because you identify only with each other?

If so, you have a mirroring friend and, most likely, are a mirroring friend yourself.

"Whenever I miss work or feel trapped at home with my daughters, I call my friends in our little cul-de-sac. They feel exactly like I do, and that helps me get through," began Meg, who lives in

Arkansas, where she and her closest friends are in the stay-at-home groove. "I don't spend much time with anyone who isn't a mother at this stage in my life. What's the point? Also, the working mothers don't really approve of me or my crowd, while the mothers who are at home, like me, understand one another. I'm the kind of person who is always trying to please everyone, and in a way, my friends who are doing what I'm doing, running ragged in the suburbs for the kids, are like that too. I try to please the friends who are in my same boat, and it makes sense. It's like we all have the same life, so when we're exhausted or our husbands are demanding on weekends or a kid has an earache the one day you planned to go shopping at the mall, you have a support system and friends to laugh with.

"I doubt that anyone who isn't in my shoes could understand. I don't feel like explaining myself to a new friend, and my friends from the past are doing different things, and we aren't exactly in synch. So I limit myself to get what's necessary and choose friends who are like me. We call ourselves martyrs, and we are."

Who hasn't had a friend who has a story like our own: issues with her mother-in-law, a boyfriend who dumped her, an extramarital affair, a wayward daughter, a promotion at work? In the **mirroring friend** we will find leaders, trophy friends, users, and frenemies who induce us; some with egotistical tendencies. Others among us, such as sharers, sacrificers, doormats, and authentic friends, have altruistic traits. What matters most is that this friend has an identity that resonates with our own. So we are drawn to her, even if we aren't the same exact kind of friend ourselves; it is the mirroring aspect of the equation that makes it work. Our mirroring friends want to be with us in good times and bad with their matching joys and sorrows (unlike misery lovers, who bolt when the sun shines again) and are able to provide great solace. So while the mirroring friend can cross with the misery lover, in the mirroring friend we find the positive and long-lasting friendships based on respect and a deep affinity for each other.

Familiar Territory

The majority of women I interviewed admitted that finding a friend whose story resonates with her own is not only soothing but a method of moving through life with new friends on the horizon. As Benedict Carey reported in his *New York Times* article "You Remind Me of Me," which ran on February 12, 2008, "immediate social bonding between strangers is based on mimicry . . . that creates a current of goodwill between two people." Subtle mimicry, Carey explains, is "instantly beguiling" because it may activate "brain circuits involved in feelings of empathy." If we apply this concept to our mirroring friends, we are mimicking their situation on some level and the empathetic feelings do reverberate.

If Meg, above, who is part sacrificer/part mirroring friend, is deeply entrenched in her surrounding group and benefiting from the effect, Jennifer, 30, who works at a newspaper and is single, believes that being part of a group distinguishes her from her old friends. In her position, the circumstances outweigh any outside influences; she is a hybrid of a doormat and a sacrificer in her endeavor.

Everyone in my business hangs out together after work and is sort of snobby. I knew when I began my job, right out of college, that it would be like this. If I resisted, I'd be shunned so fast. So I'm someone who does what everyone else does. I feel like the others do about gossip and reporters outside our circle, I'm cold to newcomers . . . it's how we are. I knew I wanted this kind of job and this kind of life for years. My friends from college and from high school have decided on very different fields, and I can't relate to what they do sometimes; even the friends who are in medical school or practicing law seem alien to me. Maybe reporters think they're really special, but I want this life, so I say, Why not? It's competitive and we work long hours and the pay isn't great, so I have to be with women who look at it the same way I do. I don't want to spend much time with anyone who doesn't get it or who isn't in the field. There is too much that's lost in translation. I want this to be direct and easy.

Since we're naturally attracted to other women who are similar to us in terms of social life, aspirations, and beliefs, we find them everywhere: at the gym, at a PTA meeting, through the workplace, children, travels, mutual friends. In a study on same-sex friendship, psychologist Marian Morry explores how these close connections are really a "projection of the self." This applies to our mirroring friendships; we relate because we are the same and the reflection of each other is in place. Consider Sarie, 22, who lives in Boston and works part-time in public relations.

I'm not sure that I've exactly "chosen" my friends, but when you grow up in a Northeastern city and go to private school, you end up meeting girls who are in the same socioeconomic group as you. After college, I'm still friends with the same people, and we do reflect one another. I'd like to think that we have more of a choice for our friendships now than in high school since there's a lot less social pressure. So the friends I choose to be with now, my close circle, are obviously people with whom I think we bring out the best in one another. In high school it was a conflict between those who had boyfriends and those who didn't. We would be critical if you spent more time with your boyfriend than with your friends. But the older we get, the more serious the boyfriend relationships become and the more legitimate they become. Today my friends and I get this. My one friend who lives with her boyfriend makes sense to me now in terms of the time she spends with him. I also have a boyfriend, so I understand prioritizing him.

We're all out looking for jobs, too, and that's another way that our lives are parallel. It's comforting to know that they're in the same place, looking for the same things. We all want to be successful and we all know it's hard and we're just starting out. Absolutely it's reassuring to be together with these friends. I have some friends who are so on track and went right to grad school or to a full-time position, and I'm proud of them, but it also makes me feel frightened in comparison. So I like to be with my friends who are also still trying to figure it out, like me.

A Variety of Circumstances

While reading Charles Frazier's novel *Cold Mountain*, I was struck by how the travesties of war rendered two disparate women lifelong friends who become reflections of each other. Ada Monroe, a minister's daughter who relocates to Cold Mountain, waits for the man she loves (and barely knows), W. P. Inman, to return from the Civil War. After Ada's father dies, Ada, alone on the farm, is introduced to Ruby, who is homeless and moves in. Under ordinary circumstances, these women wouldn't have met, let alone become close friends, but their relationship flourishes, based on a mutual need to survive and the strength they discover in each other.

Another female friendship based on unexpected mirroring is found in Lynn Nottage's play *Intimate Apparel*, which centers on Esther, a single African-American woman who works as a seamstress at the turn of the century, selling apparel to women of all walks of life. Esther's clients view her as their confidante, including Mrs. Van Buren, a white woman who is wealthy and unhappily married. The two women form a closeness and an understanding they might not have found elsewhere, in more conventional social settings. A further example about social hierarchy and a bond that develops between two women who find themselves connected is in the Argentinean film *Live-in Maid*. Norma Aleandro plays Beba, a once wealthy woman who has lost her money, and Norma Argentina plays Dora, Beba's maid. An article in *The New York Times* by Larry Rohter on July 15, 2007, "A Part Made for Her, About Life with a Maid," notes that Aleandro views the two women's worlds as parallel, describing her character and Dora as "united forever in a strange, unspoken friendship" based on "an emotional necessity and dependence."

A haunting example of negative bonds is found in Susanna Kaysen's memoir *Girl Interrupted,* about her time in a mental hospital. The friendship that begins there with Lisa, a sociopath, the toughest of the women Kaysen meets, is clearly incidental and would not have transpired in any other realm. When women feel disenfranchised from their former friends, they seek out others who are in the same position, with this as the only common thread.

Playing It Safe

This way of thinking is almost a knee-jerk response, and I recall how after my first child was born, my mother decided to introduce me to her neighbor because this woman too had a baby. We had so much to discuss, and the chance to bond was prefaced by the fact that we were both young mothers with our baby daughters in our arms. During this period of time, I'd also lost touch with some of my college friends, who mostly were not yet married and were involved with building their careers. It was a relief to make friends with someone in the same place at the same time. This substantiated the reality that friends "drift apart" or no longer get together once the link is gone. But with these changes comes another set of friends who reflect the latest stage, and the search for female connections doesn't lessen.

Too Much Information

How fortunate that you and your best friend had the opportunity to be together after college in your first jobs. Both of you moved to a new area and were starting out, and you navigated a lifestyle together. Since then you have gone through many experiences in a parallel fashion. You met and married your husbands within six months of each other and had your first babies the same year. Together you grappled with the question of working full-time versus being a stay-at-home mother. Through all of this, you have confided your innermost feelings and she has done the same.

Now that she is having marital problems, it has put you in an awkward position. She has confided a "crush" on another man, and she can't decide if she will pursue a divorce or not. It isn't that you want to take the high road but that you're uncomfortable with her confidences and her choices. It does seem that you and she are in separate universes, and it isn't as easy to be close these days. It's a loss for you, but you begin to distance yourself from her anyway, unable to adjust to the differences. She accuses you of abandoning her and not being a loyal friend, of not relating to her predicament. Is there some truth in this, you ask yourself, or is this more than you bargained for?

Balancing the connection beyond the circumstances that have brought you together can prove uneasy, as described in the composite above. Since nothing in life is stagnant, but fluid and altered by time and ongoing events, being rigid with a mirroring friend isn't a solution. However, when the new circumstance, the one that isolates you from your mirroring friend, makes you uncomfortable, the friendship is likely to suffer. For instance, Betina, 50, who lives in Maine, has recently reinvented herself in her career and finds that her one friend is very critical.

For years this best friend and I had the same life: a husband, a daughter, and success in our fields. We both loved tennis and played on Saturdays and loved going to films together. It was a safe way to be. Then I went back to school this year and decided to get a master's and apply for a teaching job. This friend thought I was crazy and kept saying, "At our age?" as if I'd done something illegal. I wanted her support, and for the first time ever, I couldn't get it. She wouldn't consider why I was tired of the same old thing and that I was being brave. So I just stopped telling her what's going on and how I feel about this change. But I hope this can im-prove, and I'm waiting for that, because we've always trusted each other, and that won't go away.

Although Betina's mirroring friend is unhappy that they are no longer threaded together, the good news is that the trust they have shared remains. The mirroring friend who devotes time and reveals herself to us is what we seek. Consider Gayla, 45, who lives in a small Southern town and works for a newspaper.

Last year I decided to get a mini face-lift and I searched for a doctor in the closest city. After I'd chosen him, I called the doctor's office to see if one of his patients would speak with me. I loved this woman, who was a city gal and sounded so sophisticated—her life was so different from mine. She knew exactly why I had to do this at 45, not 50, and why I so wanted to keep it a secret, if I could. She also told me her husband was not supportive, and I was having the same problems with my husband. I flew in a few days early, before the lift, just to meet her, and I felt like we'd be friends for life. She also looked terrific, which eased my anxiety. For some reason, I felt I could confide in this new friend and not be judged. Maybe coming from a small place means gossip is more important than keeping a friend's secret. It was great that we had no friends in common, just each other. Today we keep up and I think it's a good thing for both of us to live in two different worlds and still have so much that we understand both ways. It's sort of a bonus—my face looks better and I have a new friend who is more my soul mate than anyone for miles around me.

Mirroring at Life's Interludes

Although it is clear to us that one friend cannot fill all of our needs, when our close friends are in synch and have comparable paths, it's a plus. As I noted in Chapter 1, a group of such friends may evolve with a leader at the helm. This fits into the "common identity" theory described in Deborah Prentice, Dale Miller, and Jennifer Lightdale's "Asymmetries in Attachments to Groups and to Their Members." The authors define common-identity groups as having an attachment to the group itself—for instance, a group of female hairstylists or a group of women runners who all consider what they do to be meaningful. They compare this to common-bond groups, where the connection is among the members of the group— for example, women who are motivated to join a charity as a way to meet other women and branch out socially.

Lifelong Bonds

For three young girls who were adopted in China, Leah Potoff, Hazel Parker-Myers, and Annabelle Laserson, a mirroring friendship can be absolute. As Brooke Hauser reported in her article "Fortune's Sisters," which ran in *The New York Times* on January 6, 2008, these three girls were cribmates in the orphanage in the Anhui province of southeast China. "Before the well-tended pigtails and chin-length bobs, they wore matching institutional buzz cuts. And now, living in brownstone Brooklyn, nearly 7,000 miles away from the place they were born, they are best friends." Although no one can predict the future for these three young girls, Martha Laserson, Annabelle's mother, remarks, "There will be times when they don't want to be adopted and Chinese. But there will be other times when they need to feel adopted and Chinese. And no matter where they are, they have two other people they can talk to."

While not many of us have had such an acute link, a childhood friendship carries weight and is heartening. Consider Norris, 21, who is from Massachusetts and is presently a full-time student. Norris admitted to seeking out friends who have the same social goals and prefers a clique of friends. This attitude is based on her childhood friendships.

I couldn't be with anyone who doesn't want a moneyed life. I know it sounds superficial and as if I have no heart, but it's how I feel. I've been raised in a family that cares about this, and my younger sister is the same way. Her friends have the same lifestyle that we had and we all come from the same area of the country. My friends from growing up are like that too. We've always wanted to have friends who know, without any explaining, what we like, what we want to do. It's because we all come from the same place.

When I got to college, I only wanted to be friends with girls like me. There are four of us and we like the same boys, go to the same parties, wear the same type of clothes. The only time that my best friend and I had a problem was over a boy. She accused me of using her to get to him, and maybe I did. But she would have done it too. We're all the same, users and best friends, depending on what's going on.

While Norris reveals that she has user tendencies combined with mirroring friendships, Bett, 29, who works in retail and lives in North Carolina, seeks out coworkers who reflect her view of the world and hopes they will become social friends.

I don't want to be with someone who doesn't have the same tastes or interests as I do. Even at work, where there are lots of women, both old and young, I gravitate toward the women who remind me of myself. It doesn't matter how old they are; I care about their style. But I do want my closest friends to be my age, and if they come from the same kind of background as I do, that's a plus.

I keep up with my old friends who are on the same life plan as I am, and I want new friends like this, too; it makes it easier. At this stage, that means having a boyfriend who has a good job, getting ahead at work, knowing fashion and the right places to go at night. Anyone who is too brainy or on another path, I just don't bother with.

The Big M: Marriage

Darcie, 31, who works in real estate and lives in upstate New York, believes that her friends are obsessed with the next step in their dating lives: living together or getting married.

It used to be about who invited you to a party and who was your favorite guy, but after 29, all of my friends wanted the same thing, to settle down careerwise and also when it came to a boyfriend. In the past year, so many of my friends have gotten engaged or married, and almost everyone I know lives with someone. I feel more pressure from my friends for this to happen than I do from my mother. I've been to so many weddings in the past year, it makes me think of the movie *27 Dresses*. I'm not panicked yet, but if my friends keep getting married, I won't feel that I'm like them anymore.

Taking marriage to the next level is Mara, 37, a wife and young mother who now ponders if she will give up her career for her second child. Mara lives in the Midwest.

When my husband and I got married eight years ago, my friends in my bridal party were all married or engaged. My matron of honor was pregnant, and I knew we were on the same life plan. My best friend at work got pregnant first and I saw her struggle to decide if she should be a stay-at-home mom or a working mom. Then I got pregnant and had the same issue to face. I doubt I could be close with someone who wasn't going through this. The funny thing is, once I made the decision to go back to work, I leaned on my other best friend, who had made the same decision. Now that I'm expecting a second child, I wonder what I'll do. If I stay at home, I know I'll spend more time with the friend who has decided to give up work for her children. I just pick the friend who is most like me since it's easier and it makes me feel better, more supported.

As Mara wrestles with her decision, she exhibits doormat-like behavior, gravitating toward the friend whose stance will become hers, and her mirroring instinct seals the deal.

Divorce + Widowhood

Thankfully, the state of affairs for widows in America has been nothing like what widows in India endure. Bapsi Sidhwa's novel *Water* details how these women were cloistered in an ashram in 1938. This was the fate of widows of all ages, including eight-year-old Chuyia (married off at this tender age to an old man who dies) and Kalyani, a beautiful young woman who is forced by the leader of the ashram into prostitution, in order to generate income for this camp of widows. As distinct a collection of women as they are, the stigma of widowhood holds them together. The pecking order is complicated, survival is tricky, and the leader takes all. As in Susanna Kaysen's story, this isn't a collection of women who operate out of choice, but out of fear and lost options; the friendships aren't always pure, but they are necessary.

For Kathy, who at 47 is divorced with three children, her relationships with friends who are also divorced prove more satisfactory than do those with friends who are married.

I never thought I'd feel this way, but not only do my friends have to choose me or my ex-husband as their friend going forward, but I'm not remotely interested in friends who are doing the married thing. It reminds me of the life I no longer have, and I'd rather be with a friend who knows exactly how it is to be divorced, and what hellish situations come up. I don't feel much sympathy or understanding from my married friends, and they also act like I have some dread disease. They're so afraid that if they associate with me, they'll be divorced too. It's not so bad, really, if your marriage is terrible, to be divorced. And then there's the issue of ex-husbands and those problems. No one who is married can imagine what that's like. This is what my divorced friends know that a married friend couldn't possibly know. I need this kind of backup, I guess, so I go with the friends who have my life.

Kathy's honesty about what suits her and aids her in her divorced state also creates a shield for her. Similarly, Alice, 59, who is widowed and lives in Florida, is most comfortable in a social life with other widows.

With my girlfriend who is widowed, I'm getting what I need. If I'm with a friend who is angry about her divorce settlement or a friend who has been married for thirty years, I'm not happy. I have to be with someone like myself; I have to know I'm understood. I have tried to keep up with friends from when my husband was alive, but I know they don't want me around. Let's put it this way: I have plenty of lunch dates, but the nights are long. So I go out with my friend who is widowed. We've gotten much closer since her husband died. I remember when our kids were little, it was all about the kids, and now it's all about what we'll do with our lives and how we try so hard to keep up in a couple's world. I feel like this friend offers a lot—she goes out of her way to get tickets for shows and invites me to her club. I can't get that with a friend who isn't like me. This friend, her life is like mine. So that's where I am.

While Alice is grateful to her friend for understanding what both women endure as widows, it does make her a bit of a user (as noted in Chapter 5). According to the U.S. Census, 63 percent of the population in America today is single, and 14 percent of that group is widowed. Widows of various ages have reported that they feel maligned and mistreated, and while divorced women have described this as well, for widows, the hardship of widowhood echoes in their deliberate choices of friends and their position within the ranks.

Marissa, 52, who works in public relations and lives in Atlanta, was widowed at 40, with two young children at the time. She feels that her married friends were not that loyal after a time and she determined to find widows like herself, and to be the leader of the pack.

If I hadn't lived in a city, I'd have been out of luck, but I found other widows by networking through work friends and my neighbors, and I made us into a group. I also became the coolest widow around. I knew I had to make a new life for myself, and the friends I'd had couldn't be depended on anymore. Men don't necessarily want to date widows with young children, either. So if you have a boyfriend, he won't last. I knew about it; I was conscious of it all the time.

I wanted to be with women who felt the same, and I wanted to be in charge. I think in the end these other widows were jealous of me, and they only stayed with our group out of necessity. Like on a Saturday night when you didn't have a date, one of the widows was available, or for holidays, when your dead husband's family forgot you. Widows are treated like pariahs; there's no choice but to be with one another, even if there are contentions. I have carved this place for myself and everyone else to keep going. I've been at it for years—we shared how hard it was to raise our kids without fathers, worries about money issues . . . I was always the one with a big mouth, with strong opinions. If someone didn't like it, she still stayed; she knew it was safer than to be with married women.

Family Matters

Full Circle: Grandmothering

On a more upbeat note that applies to shared interests as the basis of a friendship, Nan, 64, who lives on the west coast of Florida, admitted that (like Alice and Marissa) she is attracted to women whose lives are like hers. Recently she has been flaunting her new status, that of grandmother.

Being a grandmother isn't that easy, although everyone acts like it is. You don't know exactly what the boundaries are and how much influence you have over your grandchildren. I have two small grandchildren, and there have been times when I feel I've pushed them too far. Maybe I've taken them out on too tiring a day, or shown them off at my office when my daughter has asked me to watch them. I have a friend who does the same thing; we're sort of competitive about our grandchildren, who gets them more, what we do with them when they're in our care. When my granddaughter was born, my friend said to me, "Just wait; this is like nothing you've ever known." And she's right, it is. She and I know something a lot of our friends don't know yet. That makes us close. Who else will listen to us boast about our grandchildren? It's really boring, unless you have a grandchild too.

The Elusive Triangle of Sisters-in-Law/Husbands/Wives

Many of us are aware of the social imperative of girlfriends forever versus frenemies (more on this in Chapter 6). In the midst of this, in what should be a comfort zone, are our circumstantial friends. But what about sisters-in-law, who are often placed in the awkward position of *having* to befriend one another, especially when the relationship can conjure up competition and jealousy? As Dotty, 37, who works as a hostess in a restaurant and lives in the South, put it, the forced companionship among sisters-in-law only ratchets up the problems.

Just because I married my husband doesn't mean I signed up for his sister to be close to me or, worse yet, a friend. I'm always thinking I have to call her if I'm going to the mall, and I take my kids over to her house when I'm on a late shift, partly because it's free babysitting and partly because I'm supposed to. But I don't like her, and I don't like how important she is to my husband and to his mother. I know they talk about me, and I know they watch every move I make. So why should I be with someone who is always out to prove me wrong, with that sick fake smile on her face? You can't escape a mother-in-law, but I don't know why I have to deal with a sister-in-law like she's someone I want to be with.

Dotty's dissatisfaction with the setup of sisters-in-law as automatic friends underscores my research for my book *Mothers-in-Law and Daughters-in-Law: Love, Hate, Rivalry and Reconciliation*. As if there isn't enough social pressure to be a good daughter-in-law or at least to pretend to be, and vice versa for the mother-in-law, the sister-in-law, who is usually a daughter-in-law's peer, is the one who appears as a friend or sisterly arrival on the scene. Then the self-serving and rivalrous aspects of the relationship surface. Consider Sheryll, 39, who lives in a small town in the Midwest and has struggled with her female in-laws for the past ten years.

Until I married into this family, I was the leader with friends—at church, at work, with my sisters. Now I'm told what to do, and my sisters-in-law and mother-in-law treat me like an outsider, like I'm second tier. They have this system of their own: The mother is at the head, but her two daughters each have their specialty. One sister hosts the holidays; the other organizes family vacations. I'm so used to making my own way and having my friends listen to me that I feel trapped. But I can escape my friends, or so I think, and I've always been able to move away from friendships when I've had enough. But here I am, in this family, where unless I get divorced, I can't leave. I'm really stuck and they're not *my* family, and not *my* friends. They're my husband's bossy sisters and bossier mother. If they were friends, I'd be gone.

While Sheryll is perturbed by the vying for the role of leader, what she resents is the prescribed "friendships" that seem an irrevocable aspect of her marriage. Yet she remains in the relationship with her sisters-in-law, unable to break free. In contrast is Barb, 44, who is a social worker and who has not spoken to her sister-in-law in years, although they were friends originally and it was she who introduced Barb to her brother.

It's odd how things turn out. Once you get into a family, it's another story altogether, and I never knew I'd be this gutsy. My relationship with my sister-in-law got lost in the family dynamic years ago and it ruined everything. I don't think anyone knows what a family is like from the outside and I doubt I would have married my husband if I'd known what pathology there is. Something had to give, and it was the friendship with my sister-in-law. I bet if I'd met her as a sister-in-law first, it wouldn't have worked, just like if we hadn't become sisters-in-law, we'd still be friends.

Welcoming the Mirror

In reading an article in the January 6, 2008, issue of *The New York Times*, "Mermaids Past and Present Keep Things Real," by Deborah Schoeneman, I was struck by how a love of the water united a young woman, Karri Holliday, 23, with her fellow mermaids, who all work as Weeki Wachee mermaids. Schoeneman wrote that mermaid culture is very popular in Aripeka, Florida, where these young women per-

form, in a four-hundred-seat glass-walled theater. One of
the mermaids, Abigale Anderson, was quoted, saying, "It's
like being in the closest sorority you could be a part of." Anderson remarked that if she meets a woman in her sixties or
seventies who used to be a mermaid, "We don't have to say
a word to each other . . . and we're hugging and bonding
over that."

Another form of mirroring that is often documented in
magazines and newspapers is that of celebrity women. These
women serve as models for everyday women, who tell me they
welcome any news at all regarding a star's battle or rivalry, as
well as intimate friendships, as a barometer for their own
lives. Therefore any positive news flashes of Nicole Kidman
and Naomi Watts, Barbra Streisand and Donna Karan,
Gwyneth Paltrow and Madonna garner our respect. According to *W* magazine, Paltrow fraternizes not only with Madonna but also with supermodel Christy Turlington Burns
and clothing designer Stella McCartney, who are described as
her "bosom buddies."

Gravitating Toward Those Most Like Ourselves

When *O, The Oprah Magazine* published an article by ZZ
Packer about her writing group of eight women, "The Finish
Party," it was described as "part boot camp, part therapy, part
lovefest." Yet the magnetism generated from how female writers support one another, joined by their profession, offering
friendship as well and the protective layer that their gather-
ings provide. As Marla Paul writes in her book *The Friendship
Crisis*, "women with strong networks of friends have bolder
immune systems, get fewer colds, and are less likely to get

cancer." Clearly the mirroring friend offers a buffer that women seek, and studies support how enticing similarities can be. On the downside, 30 percent of the women I interviewed confessed that when the mirroring friend becomes smothering or the commonality is over, they feel trapped and ready to distance themselves. Seventy percent of the women reported that they safeguarded their mirroring friends, even when circumstances change and threaten to unravel the friendship.

Calling It Quits

Does the friendship feel forced or no longer pleasurable, now that you are not on a par in your lives?

A friendship based on a mutual problem can be frozen in time, and when this happens, it's best to remove yourself, at least for the present.

Does it turn out that you don't share the same values after all?

It's a predicament when your values no longer jibe and this causes friction. Again, if the friendship is so tense and painful, it requires a break.

Successful Circumstances

Is the initial time together only the beginning of a meaningful connection?

Newfound circumstantial friends are able to forge a true closeness, beyond the initial "mirroring" phase. This is very promising for women.

Are you both growing in the friendship, even if the mirroring is no longer the same?

If you are capable of setting yourself apart, and do not need to be with women who are exactly like you, then the relationship continues. Friends respect one another's differences over time.

NINE

The Sharer: A BF in the Making

- ✗ Is your friend forgiving?
- ✗ Is she someone you trust?
- ✗ Do you confide in each other but feel she wants more?
- ✗ Would she be there in an emergency?
- ✗ Can the levels of sharing become too intense sometimes?
- ✗ Is she accountable in any situation that arises?

If your friend fits this description, she is a sharer.

"I'm so close with my two oldest friends that I don't need anyone else, and I doubt I will in the future," explained Eddie, 44, who lives in Maryland, where she is an administrator for a large company. "We tell one another so much; more than I'd tell anyone from work or someone I've met through my kids. I enjoy being with these friends—we can count on one another. I wouldn't be interested in someone I'd meet today. Our community is small, and I wouldn't reach out to anyone else but these two friends. We've confided in one another for years; no one else could ever be like this for me. I think it's the history and it's the times we've shared through the stages of our lives. It's almost like family, and I protect this—I wouldn't want anyone else to be a part of it, and I feel extremely faithful to these two friends. I guess I'm narrow-minded, and I know this group is so tight-knit. Maybe it's limiting, maybe I'm keeping myself from opportunities, but this is like a long-term marriage."

While women are known to trade confidences, the **sharer** not only will tell all but will pour herself into the friendship. The sharer remains emotional and open, friendly and focused; she *wants* you to be her best friend. This kind of friend anticipates a serious pledge from her friends and feels that she, based on her own path, can ask for it. This places her in the running for a best friend, which is the highest achievement in the realm of female friendship. A sharer, as defined by my interviewees, is: someone who listens as well as talks, who keeps in contact, who offers her thoughts, someone who isn't judging you when you confide in her, and someone who is there in a crisis and in good times. The foundation, ideally, in this context, should be sound; it is built on a virtuous plan for a personal connection. Her mantra is obvious to all: I share with you and you share back; the payoff is a secure friendship, free of game playing, rivalry, and temptation.

At the outset of the HBO series *Sex and the City*, when the four friends sat around a table confiding in one another, each had a different view of the world. Carrie was the sensible observer, Samantha was the sexually confident adventuress,

Miranda was the career woman, and Charlotte was the romantic. And it always seemed that Carrie was the link, since she was everyone's best friend. No one person in this assemblage attempted to be the leader; rather it was a mutual sharing that secured the closeness among them.

In the 2008 feature film, of the same name, each of the four friends was able to have her own trajectory while remaining a devoted friend. Although the plot centered around Carrie and how her fiancé, Big, broke her heart, the other three characters had their own "stuff" to work out, and one another to count on. This struck a chord with their audience, who identified with the sharing among the characters. Michael Cieply noted this in his article that ran on Tuesday, May 20, 2008, in *The New York Times,* "This One Goes Out to the Ladies—and Their Friends." The journalist described groups of women across the country deciding to see the film together, and planning opening-night parties for the event.

The Intricacies of Best Friendship

The sharer is good at keeping secrets, trading wardrobes, and devoting time to her closest friends for female-oriented activities. With these rituals, it is the sharer's style that shines through—it is emotional, and charged with hope and anticipation. Yet even with as promising a friend as the sharer, there can be complications. Some sharers feel they do not measure up or that they've failed a friend, despite their best intentions. Once there is a bone of contention between two close friends, a secondary characteristic of the sharer might surface, such as that of a sacrificer, a doormat, or the mirroring friend. However, in these crossover situations, the sharer remains the primary type, and her goal, of being locked in a productive friendship, remains. For example, Tory, 29, who is an attorney and lives in a Northeastern city, has been loyal to the same group since they were young.

I don't see much difference in the way my friends act today from how they acted in junior high. Now we all have jobs and are pressured at work all day, and at night, we go out. A few of my friends have boyfriends, one has a fiancé, and one has a husband, but most of them are still single. We see one another less when our love lives are in order. I talk about everything—my life is an open book.

What we try to avoid is one person outdoing the others. We all know how to do it, so we make an effort not to. This works, as long as everyone's life is okay. We're close because no one has a problem, in a way. When one of my best friends got engaged, it made everyone else sort of antsy about where they were in their lives. It's easier for us when someone blows off a boyfriend. Then we huddle together. We probably tell one another too much, and I get to be the one who cancels plans just to help get a friend through an ordeal.

Ambitious Sharers

When Tory describes her tight-knit group of sharers, what sounds ideal suffices as long as she and her friends avoid friction. In contrast, Yvette, 31, who is an office administrator in a Midwestern town, feels that the downside of too much sharing is inevitable.

I've told this friend everything at work, on a daily basis. She's been pretty understanding, and I listen to her too. There have been times when I've talked more about myself and vice versa. Who knows—it's not easy to stay together once you know so much. It can be too intense to be a best friend. And sometimes it's a drain, all this confiding and being on top of each other's lives. I was always told by my mom and her friends to have a friend like this, and to treasure the relationship. If something goes wrong at work or with a boyfriend, the first thing you do is turn to your closest friends. They're supposed to be there, and one special friend is the one who helps get you through it. Maybe I don't question this enough since I don't know another way to go about it, even when it gets too heavy. What I'm saying is that being this person or leaning on her is a heavy burden.

The skinny on the sharer is that we are *encouraged* to have these wonderful, feel-good relationships with women, and anything less makes us think that we have failed. For this reason, it is a constant search for such a best friend, despite any strong nullifying elements. For example, Deidre, 54, who works in design and lives in Nevada, has struggled with unhappy experiences with her closest friends.

I've been at this for years, having such a close girlfriend and having a man in my life and feeling like I have to choose. At first I was too naive to realize it wasn't good for me; it wasn't healthy. I remember how I'd spend time with my best friend, and we'd tell each other all about a boyfriend, or our husband, as it were. Then I'd leave this friend and I'd feel so bad about the man. I'd go home to my partner and he could tell that I'd been with that friend, just by how my attitude toward him had changed, due to her influence. Usually it was so negative that after a while, I started to think maybe this wasn't such a good idea, to be mixing it together. Sure, we were supposed to be so close, but it was spilling over to my romantic life in a negative way and I was unhappy with both the friend and the guy. That's when I realized I had to be careful, and to not confide in a girlfriend to the point where it had an effect on my love life. It got so that I let go of a few women friends, and some of them had been there for years.

Mixed Signals

Our society encourages close friendships among women, but we're also taught to be wary of one another, *to trust and mistrust*. With this double-talk, which begins early in our lives and creates confusion, it's no wonder we seek out friends and at the same time withhold data. The sharer is supposed to be the friend with whom we become close and have a successful relationship. But often enough, as we have witnessed in earlier chapters, there are painful episodes and a friend can be disingenuous.

Too Much Too Soon

Women describe wanting to get close very fast, and then perceiving a slight from the friend, real or imagined, which becomes a problem. Patti, 39, who recently moved to Kansas and works for an airline, admitted that she forces a closeness with some of her friends.

I'm the one who pushes for this closeness. Maybe I do it to feel protected since I moved here just a few years ago. I thought if I had a friend I really trusted and we could count on each other, I'd be in a better position. So I pushed for this friend to be my best friend, to be very special and to go beyond the others. That worked for a while, but I think I'm too demanding and that I get sort of crazy if I don't think she's paying enough attention to me.

That's why it's so strange that now I'm the one with new friends, when this friend would have been happy to escape how intense our friendship was. I've made some friends at the gym and I know it's threatening to how close my best friend and I are, but I'm having fun. I find myself making excuses rather than telling her I have plans with this new group. It's like I'd rather cheat on her than confront her. If she did this to me, I'd go nuts—I'm starting to get really close with a new friend.

Patti's take on her friendship and her decision to move away emotionally after expecting so much of her first best friend shows us how skittish a woman can be. If a woman's plan is to trade insider information with whomever she seeks out, it is almost as if the objects of her affection are fungible. Then her way of treating every friend is the same, regardless of who the recipient is.

The Overrated Experience

Part of the issue for sharers, those who take themselves as seriously as does Eddie (whom we met at the start of this chapter), is that these relationships have their own tempo and cannot always be controlled. Thus, we see how the stages and changes in our lives affect our closest friendships, as documented in Chapter 8, "The Mirroring Friend." Once a sharer feels she has invested so much of herself in the friendship that it has to be exclusive, it can be a burden for the recipient. Occasionally a sharer will seek a confidante outside her usual circle of friends, in order not to be judged, and a closeness can develop beyond the prescribed social strata.

Thus was the friendship that evolved between Mary Todd Lincoln and Elizabeth Keckley, a freed slave and talented dressmaker whom Mary hired during Lincoln's presidency. According to Jean Baker in her biography, *Mary Todd Lincoln*, despite their dissimilar backgrounds, in Mrs. Keckley Mary found someone whom she could trust with her sorrows and the overwhelming trials of being First Lady during the Civil War. Although Mrs. Keckley was a strong, independent woman who had bought her freedom and whose son had died in the war, it was Mary's sadness that prevailed in the relationship. Mrs. Keckley was the sharer/sacrificer/doormat who was there for Mary when the Lincolns' son died in the White House. Mrs. Keckley was called to come to Mary's side on the night that Lincoln was shot. The end to the friendship occurred when Mrs. Keckley published a book that Mary considered a betrayal of shared secrets.

How the Sharer Materializes

The movie *Legally Blonde,* starring Reese Witherspoon as Elle Woods, exhibits another unlikely friendship that develops between sharers, with Witherspoon's character's needs taking precedence. When Elle Woods leaves her comfortable sorority life behind to attend Harvard Law School, she's snubbed by the female students. In despair, she finds a manicurist who listens to her travails and eases her pain. Elle ends up sharing all the details of her life with this woman, played by Jennifer Coolidge, who in turn offers an honest friendship. And she gets to complain about her own life, too, soliciting Elle's understanding in return. In this case, the rewards of the friendship are in balance.

As Dr. Ronnie Burak points out, there are those who can and those who cannot handle the friend who tenders too many of her troubles. "Sure, it's true that a friend wants to please and help but she can be taken advantage of by the needy friend. If the rescuer/pleaser gets her self-esteem by caring for the needy person, it can be okay. If she's too encumbered, she'll move away." Consider Michaela, 39, who works as an executive and lives in Virginia. Recently she decided to distance herself from a friend who shared too many details of her divorce.

Maybe I was flattered for a moment, but then I didn't want to be part of my friend's dissolving marriage. I had enough after a few weeks, and the divorce dragged on for years. I had to be her booster since we were such good friends, but she really pushed me too hard. Whatever I had to confide, it wasn't newsworthy or juicy or dramatic, it was just life as usual—money, kids, husband. Hers was this big deal, and I got so tired of it that I moved away from her emotionally and ended up not being a very good friend. She was calling five times a day and telling me things I'd already heard and it was too much. I have a job and a life. I didn't have the guts to not be her friend, but it was clear to her that I wasn't going to be the best person to tell all to. That's how I dealt with it, by being too busy with my own life to possibly take care of hers. We're still friends, but I do notice that she's friendlier now with other divorced women and with people she's met since her divorce. That's better; we were so separate after a while.

Unlike Michaela, who purposely set limits, is Justine, 48, who works in real estate and lives in the Southwest. Justine has noticed a strain between her and her best friend as of late but is reluctant to act on it.

She's a friend because we were friends for so long. It was all fun until we had our children, and then what I shared with her about my daughter became a kind of competition based on how perfect her daughters are. That started years ago, when we were really close. She had been the sexy one and the one who was out there, and there's been this sort of ongoing competition. But we always told each other everything and we were very interlocked. People thought we were sisters, we were that close. Now it feels tense, and maybe it's my fault. What's slipping away is the sharing—maybe because I don't put more effort into it. I'm relieved and also sorry. I miss being close, but I don't miss feeling like there's something between us, like I'm walking on eggshells. So I stick around without saying all this.

Rescuers to the Front

Like the doormat, the sharer evolves early and is highly defined by junior high. The sharer is in search of her constituents, always hopeful that a reciprocity exists. This takes the sharer through college, where her abilities are honed, and although she makes new friends, she hangs on dearly to her old friendships as well. It is more likely that the sharer, whose intentions are pure, unlike the leader, the user, the frenemy, and the trophy friend, will attach herself to friends for the long haul. Part nature, part nurture, the sharer (who can also be a sacrificer, a doormat, or an authentic friend) is almost overbearing to the friend with whom she shares and, in a way, stymies the relationship. For Donna, 41, who lives in a Southern state, where she works at a marina, this scenario is all too common.

I put all this energy into my best friend, in my opinion, and I'm sure she thinks I'm not there for her. This has been going on for quite some time, and once in a while I consider chucking the whole thing. It's not her fault, it's mine, but there's such tension in the relationship because I can't do what she does for me. First it was my abusive husband, and then it was my messed-up kid, and she was ready to take it on. Not only was she there, but she was willing to give time and to say she knew my pain because of what she'd been through with her daughter. She got me to go to AA meetings, which meant she had to tell me what was wrong with her kid, and she took that risk. It's not easy to show what's really going on in your life when it's so unhappy. She even picked me up and took me home afterward. And still it's hard for me. I feel like she's always waiting for me to do as much as she's done, to tell her as much as she's ready to tell me. I'm not as good a friend.

Quid Pro Quo

Although she is willing to share, Donna is not a sharer by nature, or not at the level of her best friend, to whom she feels indebted. Similarly, Christina, 29, who is a graduate student living in the Northeast, feels that she is not as constant as her best friend, who shares on an ongoing basis.

I don't want to be pressured all the time by this perfect friend. I'm sure I've disappointed her over time. I know she thinks I owe her for all she's done by being such a total friend. I ended up moving to the same town she'd moved to after college. She put her boyfriend and her work to the side to help me get settled. She really took time and put some thought into how to make it easier for me. This friend introduced me to her friends, had a small party for me. I didn't do much to thank her, besides buying her dinner one night and returning her calls. She acts like I'm as good a person as she is, but I doubt she really believes it. I always have work and am in the library and say that I can't join her. She's done nothing but reach out to me and try to introduce me to people she knows and show me around.

The Glitches

Okay, so we all know the upside of the sharer and the struggle for her object of affection to feel that she has credibility and is as solid a citizen herself. We understand the weight of giving back to the sharer and falling short and how this looms large for some women. But what about the demanding side of the sharer, those qualities that make her trying at times?

Burning Out Close Friends

At first the nature of the sharer is nothing short of impeccable, and the recipient is thrilled to be in such company. Eventually, though, the sharer can become unrelenting if she's displeased with the lack of response from her friends.

As Dennie, 48, who lives and works part time in Florida, recalled:

I was too stupid to realize I'd had enough of this friend. She'd become snappish and intolerant, all because I couldn't be as good and kind to her as she was to me. It made me start to move away; I couldn't even appreciate her after a while.

Triangles and the Sharer

The sharer is best in pairs, and a threesome is not necessarily welcome, but she will do the best she can if the occasion arises. Still, what can take the sharer over the top is when this threesome upsets her equilibrium, since she is the giving one who puts effort into the relationship.

Tracey, 25, who lives in Mississippi and works at a hotel, views herself as too responsible to her group of friends.

I was the one who danced in circles. It was hard to penetrate how cliquish they were, and I was so eager to please, so willing to share my room, my clothes—I'd even change my work schedule for them. Maybe what my stepmother taught me is right: Two's company, three's a crowd. I was finally over it, over trying for them.

Lenders and Borrowers

If the world is divided into these two types, it is the sharer who is willing to lend and hesitant to borrow. Still, she expects something back and will eventually tire of the borrower unless there is a convincing gesture made in her direction.

For Alexandra, 39, who lives in Southern California and works in fashion, being a lender is a way to reach out to her closest friends.

I do it for me. I let my close group of friends use my clothes, purses, shoes, even jewelry on special occasions. I joke that I could have a side business doing this, but I don't charge—and I could, since I have access to some great fashion-forward clothes through work. After a while it bothers me that no one makes any gesture toward me. This is a favor and I would like a favor back.

In contrast to Alexandra is Jolie, 21, who is a full-time student living in Arkansas. Jolie considers herself a borrower, not a lender.

I'm not a good sharer, and I have a lot of things I wouldn't let a friend use. I don't like sharing my things, and I never have. No one can use my purse or book bag or coat. And I borrow coats, hats, books, whatever, from friends if I need to. I'm not that careful about returning them. It's just that the friends who lend their things don't mind and I would always mind.

Divulging Secrets: Traitorous Acts

If the sharer has spilled her guts and now she and her confidante are estranged, the greatest betrayal is if that friend spreads her secrets. Not only does it end the relationship, but the thought that it *might* happen gnaws at the sharer's very center and creates anxiety.

Nadia, 45, who lives in upstate New York and works as a landscaper, had left a friend and then reconnected with her over a secret.

It was hard for me to be in this relationship once I thought she had told my other friend what I'd disclosed to her. I feel I've been very loyal and aboveboard, and I don't know why she'd tell my story to someone else. It took me years to become her friend again. I did it because we had history together and I wasn't able to let that go. I know what she did and I want to be her friend anyway.

Unexpected Obstacles: Children

Ironically, what brings women together can also tear them apart. When women meet as mirroring friends through their children and a few sharers emerge, it may work initially, only to crumble over time. As the children grow apart, so can the mothers, including those with the best intentions.

Priscilla, 40, who lives in South Dakota, is beginning to realize that her daughter's falling-out with her best friend has hurt Priscilla's relationship with the mother.

I was the giving one in this friendship, and it was about the girls and *not* about the girls. That is, until our girls got to high school and her daughter got into trouble. Then I was asked to go beyond the call of duty for my friend, covering up for her daughter—lying just like the mother did. And I don't want my daughter to be influenced by this girl. So I've stopped reaching out; I've gotten sort of cold and unfriendly.

The Sharer's MO

As Steven Pinker pointed out in his article "The Moral Instinct," which ran in *The New York Times Magazine* on January 13, 2008, "Fairness is very close to what scientists call reciprocal altruism, where a willingness to be nice to others can evolve as long as the favor helps the recipient more than it costs the giver and the recipient returns the favor when fortunes reverse." Pinker then explained how the brain addresses these "moral emotions": Sympathy induces a favor; anger shelters the giver so that she will not tolerate the "cheater" who takes the favor and does not repay the friend; this is followed by gratitude, then guilt, which causes the "cheater" to promise better results next time.

If we apply what Pinker addressed in his article to the sharer's experience, it appears that she is frequently upset with a lack of exchange. Meanwhile, non-sharers, who are thrilled to have a sharer in their lives, may feel grateful toward her *and* guilty for not doing as much in return. Consider Debbie, 50, who lives in Kansas, where she is retired as a manager for a company. Widowed with two grown daughters, Debbie is aware that her best friend takes her for granted.

I try to be a good friend, and it's my goal to do all that I say I'll do, but there are times when my best friend has taken advantage. Meanwhile, I've always put myself on the back burner for her, and now I'm about to change. A few months ago, I had serious health problems, but I got out of my bed to help her since she's been sick for longer. That's when I ended up in the hospital. Still, she's spoiled by me, and I'm in the process of unspoiling her, letting her know how it is. She did and didn't appreciate my effort, and I doubt she'd share herself the same way. The thing is, she heard me and knows how I feel now. Even when she hurts my feelings, I'd never abandon her.

In contrast to Debbie's reaction to her friend's lack of appreciation is Luella, 40, who lives in Michigan and works as a freelance artist. Luella confesses to being on the receiving end of her friend's endeavors.

I sometimes feel terrible that she does so much for me, and other times I remind myself that this is how she is; she likes being the giver. Maybe I expect too much from her, but I get it, don't I? She's the one who takes the time to visit me, and when I had the flu she brought over soup and cooked my son dinner. She seems to like it, and I usually do too, unless I'm honest with myself that there's not much giving back on my end. Sometimes I actually think this friend needs better boundaries, but that's her, not me. I'm certain we're in it for the long haul.

With both Debbie, as a sharer/sacrificer, and Luella, at the other end of the spectrum, we see what transpires in terms of tension and distance between friends, based on a lack of return. What is notable is that as conscious as each woman is of how she is positioned in the relationship, neither is willing to lose the friend.

Risk/Reward Ratio

Although a female best friend is a romantic notion, and losing this friend can pierce one's heart, there are also practical reasons behind the union. However we find this person, the best friend is of utmost importance, and women do not take this connection lightly. To cultivate this kind of relationship has risks, yet women gladly do it for the reward. The longing for a best friend to share with is a big part of the picture for women of all ages, whether married, in a long-term relationship, or single. Among my interviewees, over 80 percent of the women expressed this sentiment and, as a result, found themselves making adjustments to preserve the relationship.

Standing by Your Friend

When it comes to the sharer, there is little self-illusion since, for the most part, what she offers her friends is positive, and her willingness is genuine. The sharer hopes to find, as we have noted, an appropriate level of reciprocity in her friend's actions. A happy tale regarding this ratio is in the film *Juno*, starring Ellen Page as Juno, a 16-year-old who unexpectedly finds herself pregnant and decides to have the baby. Juno's best friend, Leah, played by Olivia Thirlby, is at first shocked but adjusts quickly and exhibits great maturity as a friend. Leah stands by Juno when she announces her news to her parents, she tells Juno all that she hears about the father of the child (a classmate), and she is there to coach Juno during the delivery. When we think of best friends going the distance, Leah faces ridicule from fellow schoolmates for her association with Juno and, more profoundly, the challenges of holding on to a friend whose life is altered forever.

Time and Energy

The sharer and her best friend are keenly conscious of the qualities needed for these connections to succeed. Because friendship is entwined with the constraints of time, this aspect of friendship is treated with respect by the sharer. In our frenetic lives we each strive to have enough time for ourselves, let alone our spouse/significant other, children, parents, work, and friends. A majority of the women I spoke to confessed to placing their friends second to their other obligations, yet it is the sharer who somehow manages to incorporate her friend into her tight schedule.

Another quality both sought and offered by the sharer is energy. Although not everyone has the same energy level, the sharer specifically allots energy to her friends, just as she does time. This manifests in applying serious thought to a friend's problem, choosing a great birthday celebration for a friend, easing a friend's stress level when the friend is in dire straits. Alex, 22, who works in film production in Los Angeles and is a part-time student, reflected on the energy quotient.

I think that my friends and I feed off each other, and everyone has a preference for a certain kind of energy level. It's just the kind of person you want to be with—for me, not too bubbly and not too flat, but someone I understand. Then we can be energetic for each other—it all depends on the friendship, and then we do things for each other and we have this common ground.

Possessions and Money

The third quality that sharers offer applies to possessions and financial status. Sharers are by nature open to loaning out their possessions (see "Lenders and Borrowers" earlier in this chapter). This mentality is not limited to clothing and accessories; a sharer will also extend herself to help a friend, which is where the energy kicks in. If a friend needs a place to stay in another city, the sharer will go out on a limb, asking a friend or a cousin located there to put the friend up. The sharer is willing to loan you her car, laptop, CD collection, a real piece of jewelry, without any caveat, and with real trust. One interviewee said that when her child needed surgery, one of her best friends offered to donate blood when they were in search of donors.

A primer on how the concepts of time, energy, and money are interwoven in female friendship is exhibited in the feature film *Friends with Money,* starring Jennifer Aniston, Catherine Keener, Joan Cusack, and Frances McDormand. Aniston's character, Olivia, is at a crossroads and looks to her three best friends, played by the above-referenced actresses, for financial and emotional support. However, each of these friends, all of whom appear to be more settled than Aniston's character, has her own level of unhappiness that limits her ability to be supportive. Aniston's character, who still wants for affection, does the best, on some level, with the attempts of Joan Cusack's character, Franny, to be the sharer. The film also drives home how much one's moneyed life, or lack thereof, affects a friendship.

A friendship that evolves among three unlikely women, is featured in another film, *Mad Money,* starring Diane Keaton as Bridget, a middle-class wife; Queen Latifah as Nina, a single mother; and Katie Holmes as Jackie, a young, unencumbered woman. The three women, who all work at the Federal Reserve Bank in Kansas City, bond when Bridget decides they should rob the bank. When they are caught, Holmes's Jackie offers to take the rap for Nina, so that she can stay with her sons and not go to prison. These two films highlight how the best intentions of the sharer can be waylaid for her own personal dramas— romance, marriage, children, work, financial woes.

The Currency of the Sharer

Although the intimacy might be too encumbering for some, according to the professionals referenced in this chapter,

the sharer is highly valued amid the intricacies of life for
women. This is confirmed by the percentages who are committed to this friend—45 percent of those who are sharers
themselves view this kind of friendship as a way of life;
40 percent of those who are sharers view it as a drain
but stick it out. Only 10 percent describe their role as sharer
as too intense, and 5 percent who are recipients leave a
sharer.

Has your friend ever thanked you for your efforts on her behalf?

For the sharer, there are psychic rewards for being such a
caring friend. Thus, a true sharer is not deterred by a lack of
gratitude and does not give up if she isn't acknowledged, as
long as there is enough communication that she *knows* she is
appreciated.

As a sharer, do you have a threshold?

Even a devoted best friend can say "enough" if her friend is a
user, a misery lover, or, on occasion, a leader. For those
sharers who feel they've been used and have sacrificed too
much, there is a limit. It is sometimes best to take a break
and focus more on yourself and the reciprocal relationships in
your life.

As the friend of the sharer, can you repay her for her constancy?

If you can give your sharer, as a token of appreciation, tickets
to a concert or a special gift, this will go a long way in terms of
making her feel secure in the friendship.

Do you ever feel less than your sharer, as if you won't measure up?

When the sharer is an impeccable friend, it is hard to not feel as if you don't give enough back. A heart-to-heart about your feelings might help, and an honest evaluation of what you bring to the table as a friend is also helpful.

TEN

The Authentic Friend: The Real Deal

✗ Is your friend truly empathetic?
✗ Can you count on her in any circumstance?
✗ Does she know her bounds?
✗ Can you lose touch after months or years and pick up again immediately?
✗ Do you have the same worldview?
✗ Does it matter if you do not have the same worldview?

If your friend fills the bill, you are blessed with an authentic friend.

"I doubt I would have become friends with my best friend from graduate school if I hadn't been so far from home," said Gia, 36, who works in the food industry and lives in Kansas. "She seemed too snobby to me and unfriendly at first. But we were living near each other on this large campus and were thrown together enough that we ended up friends. I thought she was spoiled, and she was. But that didn't mean she wasn't a good friend to me, someone I got to know and care about, although at first impression, I never imagined that would be the case. I believe that I sort of pigeonholed her until I got to know her, thinking that anyone from a big city on the East Coast had to have airs. That's not true, once you learn about her, and that's what matters. She's so easygoing, and that's what I like. I'm actually more set in my ways, but I've learned to bend some too because of her."

And so, the final chapter brings us to the **authentic friend**, the one we are in search of, a woman who has a high tolerance for her friend's entanglements and is deeply committed to the relationship. This relationship makes it worth all the ups and downs inherent in female friendship, and operates on mutual self-esteem, care, and flexibility. This is the friend who reinvents her role and adapts as friendships alter with time; she also remains steadfast with the patterns that have succeeded over the years. Among the types of friends, this is the one we cherish; she is sincere, earnest, and doesn't wonder what is in it for her. This is the friend worth keeping— she offers empathy and support, even when her life or her friend's life is in disarray.

It can be a sleight-of-hand to ease such a genuine friendship into the constant turmoil of our personal lives in the twenty-first century. In the previous chapters we have witnessed the degrees to which a friend disappoints us or stands up to our expectations and, in either case, the entanglement of the relationship. In both cases, women repeatedly express their hopes for satisfying friendships. As Gabrielle Leblanc points out in her article in *The Huffington Post* on April 4, 2008,

"5 Things Happy People Do," women spend much of their time involved with activities they don't like. A friend should, ideally, provide a reprieve from the tedium and responsibilities that seem to engulf us, a pathway to contentment.

Hitting Your Threshold

Adair, 44, who is a nurse and lives in the Midwest, believes that age makes us wiser to both our pleasing friends and our inadequate ones.

I don't have much goodwill anymore for my friends who take advantage or who disappoint me. I feel like I've started sorting through people, and the ones who don't fit get tossed out—I think I've found my limit. But the ones who fit, they matter to me now more than ever before. Now that I'm over forty, it isn't just about running after kids or trying to make some money. Not that this doesn't matter, but my friends are the ones I count on for the happier times. For women it just keeps changing, what makes us happy. First it's supposed to be your lover, then your children, and finally your friends. It's as if you didn't have real friends when you were distracted by family and other commitments. Once that fades away—and it does—it's the women friends who matter most.

Fortunate Encounters

Originally you met this woman through business and lost touch. Six years ago, you rediscovered each other when your sons ended up in kindergarten together. As two working mothers in the same field, you were thrilled to be reunited. You began to plan playdates for the boys and would e-mail each other in the evening. The friendship was progressing nicely, and it felt more genuine to be with this friend than with many of your friends from college or childhood. Somehow this wasn't competitive, nor was it a power play. You felt that she had your best interests at heart, and you returned the sentiment.

When you decided to get divorced, you knew that she was next before she did. But it wasn't that you had to be in the same boat to be close, it was more that you saw her more clearly than she saw herself in some ways. You felt that you would support whatever came next in her life and that you had her support in return. The boys continued to be friendly, and this worked well when she was dating and her son needed a sleepover. For a time, when you had a love interest, this friend reciprocated. Every summer you plan a week's vacation together, and it is always a pleasure. Recently, you decided to begin a small business with her and you have the utmost confidence that it will work, in terms of trust and how sound the concept is. This friendship has enhanced your life, and you are closer to this friend than to almost anyone outside your immediate family.

The Effort It Takes

The amalgam above is a glowing recommendation of how a "perfect" friendship can play out. But for so many of us, this is a pipe dream. Female friendships are nuanced; women frequently wonder where our genuine connections will come from.

With the authentic friend, there is an upbeat quality that

we don't always find in the other scenarios. Women describe this as a buffer against the world, as if they are safer because of these treasured friendships. Below are the most common ingredients found when the friendship works.

The Ability to Give and to Reciprocate

As corny as this sounds, it isn't easy to find a friend who can pull this off. Although we might expect that certain friends will be generous of spirit, the only ones to count on, besides the authentic friend, are the sacrificer, who would go out on a limb for her friend in need; the sharer, since she yearns for the closeness; and the mirroring friend, in a "we do for each other" rhythm. It remains tricky when the doormat acts as if she's going to give back, and since she is fairly benign, we fall for it, although by nature this person might not be so inclined. Or the trophy friend fools us into thinking she is devoted, when she is not, while the leader makes it clear from the outset that giving is not in her repertoire. The frenemy and the user do not even come into play in this capacity.

Liza, 49, who works in a research lab in a Northeastern city described herself as part sharer/part mirroring friend. The sense of security that Liza finds with her authentic friend is a tremendous boost.

This friend and I do well together. We cover for each other with our kids, our elderly parents, our work schedules, and we help each other out. It's almost like we speak a special language, and there's a comfort zone I can't find anywhere else. We're totally devoted. Maybe it's because our lives are so parallel, but I think it goes beyond this. I can't imagine a time when we won't be there and as close as we are now. We tell each other everything; it's not like any other friendship.

The Courage to Be Honest

Women can lie to themselves about large and small issues in relationships when things aren't going well. With a frenemy, a misery lover, or a user, the lies are often bold-faced, and told to their friends for personal gain. The mirroring friend is also capable of being disingenuous, looking you in the eye and offering a fib if it suits the occasion. The sacrificer will skirt being honest at times, while the doormat might be too needy to be anything but truthful, and figures honesty is the best policy. The leader lies to retain her power—so we are left with the sharer and the authentic friend, whose level of obligation to her friends preempts the lie, even in times of strife.

Terri, 31, who is a teacher and lives in Florida, believes that her best friend has made some wrong decisions that have affected her. She also knows that her friend cares about her, so she forgives her.

When I was dating a man my best friend disliked, she tried to keep him away from me. Since we are roommates, she took his calls sometimes, and when he called on our landline, she erased the messages. A few times when he e-mailed me and my screen was up she read his e-mails, then deleted them. I doubt she should have done this, but I know she was trying to help me out. I found out about all of it later on, when I'd met my new boyfriend, who is now my fiancé.

I suppose she did the right thing in steering me away from my old boyfriend, but she also tampered with information and kept things from me. What kind of friend is that? Someone who cares so much that she makes these decisions for you? I would have done the same, though I'd rather talk about it with the friend, try to sort things out that way. Today I'm engaged to someone else and I think her decision helped make this possible. So how can I hold it against her?

The Offer of Stability (Belief in the Tried-and-True)

Stability becomes a primary factor in these friendships, and there is a high success rate among women friends who feel committed, for better or for worse. In contrast to the friend who describes her friendship as a safe haven are those women who feel unsafe but stuck in an unrewarding friendship. Different women recognize security in different friends; the sacrificer reports finding solace in belonging to a group and seeks out a leader, the doormat isn't responsive enough at times, and the user and the misery lover, women say, may ooze an ersatz sense of security, but this dwindles over time. Mirroring friends reflect the other's need to feel protected, and find it within the relationship, as long as they remain similar. The frenemy and the trophy friend are not signed on for this quality in friendship.

Consider Allie, 36, who works at a restaurant and recently reunited with her high school best friend.

We've been separated by three thousand miles for long enough for me to know we have to make an effort, both of us. I'm single while she's married with kids, so it's not about that—in fact, that's what makes it hard to be friends, how our lives are so dissimilar. But we were friends long ago when life was less stressful and crazy. We really meant it, and that feeling just doesn't go away. I don't want us to give up again. I have enough phony friends to know she matters. This friend makes me feel protected—maybe because we have this past together, we know each other so well.

Forgiveness and Acceptance

Whatever your lifestyle and personal situation, it is the friend who doesn't judge you who is the bona fide friend. Interviewees said they felt friction in their friendships, particularly with the trophy friend, the misery lover, and the user, over their decisions. The leader and the mirroring friend often set a positive tone, the doormat is accommodating by nature, while the sharer, the sacrificer, and the authentic friend are excellent at forgiveness and acceptance. What women want is recognition for their actions and choices. Dr. Donald Cohen points out why being supportive of our friends works: "Women want to be caretakers and have a strong mothering instinct and can be very open-minded. The women who take charge need to be needed and also benefit from having others follow."

When it comes to gathering and confessing, Tammy, 60, a leader and an authentic friend, is a pro. She lives in a Southern city, where she works in sales and has an assortment of close friends.

I gather my closest friends together like a litter of kittens, and every one seems so needy. I'm the one firing up their enthusiasm, getting them to go on retreats, to restaurants, to parties. But it's not that easy. At my age, I'm not worried about any bickering or jealousies anymore, or who has what; I'm more concerned about shepherding everyone from one event to the next. It can be super-

ficial at times, unless someone has a crisis, and then we're all
there. Sometimes we tell one another what we've done that de-
serves forgiveness; it's almost like we absolve one another. We listen to one another's problems and try to figure out what would
help. It works for me, too; I have this one set of friends, and we're
locked in.

Shared Values

Ultimately it is the authentic friend who gets us through the
tough times, and without her at our side (literally or virtually),
we can feel misunderstood. We know that mirroring friends
have shared values based on common circumstances, while
for the sharer, it's all about her focus on the relationship. As
much as the sacrificer wants to be like her friends, she can be
comfortable with not having the same principles and view it
as an expression of individuality. The doormat, of course, will
take on the moral code of her closest female friends, while the
leader does not consider this of utmost importance—either
way, the relationship suffices for her. The trophy friend will
analyze how much this means to the woman she lures, and
put it into play if necessary. The user and the frenemy invari-
ably do not have shared values with their close friends, nor is
it a factor for either of these types.

Anne, 50, who works part-time as an occupational therapist
and lives in a Northeastern city, believes that friends with the
same basic outlook are compelling.

My philosophy is that as a daughter, a mother, an aunt, and a
sister, I can only have easy friends, who look at life the way I do.
With all the expectations put on me, I have to love and accept my

friends, and get the same from them. A friend who brings problems doesn't fit, and I dumped that type a long time ago. A lot of my friends are divorced, and I am too. So we end up spending time together. And sure we're in the same boat, but we also look at life the same way. The friends who dropped me when I got divorced aren't my real friends to begin with. I have met so many amazing women since I've become single, and these are my closest friends.

Empathy and Caring

Dr. Barton Goldsmith remarks, "Honest relationships are hard to come by, and a woman who is able to genuinely offer empathy is the authentic friend. This is what we hope for." Having empathy for our friends requires the same amount of effort as does spreading negative energy. The types of friends who are most caring and have the most affinity for this include the authentic friend, who can cross with the doormat, who absorbs her friend's problems; the sacrificer, who is trustworthy with her friend's secret or issue; and the sharer and the mirroring friend. The misery lover feels that her friends are measured against her own situation, while a user and or a trophy friend can *appear* empathetic, or will be in the moment, in a self-serving mode that has limits. The frenemy is not interested in helping out or trying to fathom a friend's pain, unless it feeds into the rivalrous aspect of the relationship.

Consider Sarah, 25, who lives in Los Angeles, where she is a graduate student.

I have six close friends; we all went to college together. One of them is a leader, and she organizes everything and has kept us all in touch. We have different personalities and can be a bit like bickering sisters. But we aren't competitive and we really care what is happening to one another. We absolutely trust one another, and it's a very nondramatic group, basically built around a history of where we each come from and where we're trying to go in our lives. What is for sure is how much we feel for one another in any crisis or when there's good news to share.

As evidenced by the stories in this chapter, those who have achieved authentic friendships and those who have not are equally aware that steadfastness, ongoing respect, and magnanimity are at a premium when they succeed.

Setting Limits

What I found in interviewing women for this book is how often a friend will overstep bounds. Establishing boundaries with friends has been an issue throughout many long-standing friendships, since there is no standard to follow when it comes to how we engage and express our intimate feelings. So while Terri, whom we met earlier in this chapter, feels gratitude for her friend's actions, Nancy, 51, who lives out West, feels that her close friend was wrong to interfere with her affairs.

My son hadn't spoken to me for months, and my closest friend met with him and sort of took his side. I didn't know about it until after the fact, but I feel she took advantage and wasn't thinking of my best interests. She knew how much I was troubled by his not coming around. So I told her I was angry and felt violated, but because I wanted to still be friends, I didn't break it off. I think she really wanted to help, that she was sincere, but she made a mistake. For me it was about what was good here and what she had done and where you draw the line. I wouldn't have done this to her, and it was hurtful. Did she have the best intentions? I have to think so in order to go ahead with the friendship.

My Girlfriend's Back: Reuniting with Long-Lost Friends

No one knows how a friend will weigh in during a crisis, although we think we can predict her response. What we hope for is our friend's support and loyalty. When I asked women about this, over 50 percent said that with their best friend, there had been a level of disillusionment at some point during an ordeal. The other half felt that their friend had been their savior and had gotten them to the other side. Yet for over 70 percent of my interviewees, an old friend from childhood or college days who reappeared offered solace that is not found in newer and more circumstantial friendships made later in one's life. Consider Patti, 56, who is an artist and lives in New Mexico. Her reunion with a friend from high school has been most rewarding.

I was concerned and disappointed not to hear from this friend for years. Then she came to New Mexico and we got together. I think maybe she'd been depressed and hadn't wanted me to know. When I had reached out to her during that time, she didn't want to talk about it. Now she seems on track, although both of us have been knocked around quite a bit by life. Maybe that's why being in touch is so meaningful to me—we remember how it was and we *know* each other. From the second we got together, it was as if all these years hadn't gone by. And with her back in my life, I feel better, more understood. I really regret the time that passed when we weren't in touch. But that won't happen again.

Although Patti's situation is satisfying, there are times when a cog in the works is inevitable. This can happen in the best of friendships and after a prolonged separation. As Anita, 40, who is a physician who lives in Northern California, views it, some things never change.

At first being in touch with this friend from summers at the beach was so exciting. We had lost touch and then ran into each other and worked hard at getting together. It reminded me of being in love again—like finding my old boyfriend. We had so many of the same memories and we were still the same, although it had been years since we'd really spent time together. During this period, my ex got sick, and I was doubly relieved to be in touch with my friend. When that crisis ended and he was okay, she sort of disappeared. Just like she had done in high school and when we were young and single. Suddenly, I remembered it all, and it was so disappointing since I do still think of her as a special friend, a real friend. She just hasn't shaken her pattern. I think she's her own worst enemy.

As with Anita's experience in real life, the middle-aged women friends in Ann Packer's novel *Songs Without Words*, go into a tailspin when their friendship is threatened. Packer's characters' best friendship is tested when they find themselves in an unexpected predicament. In this modern-day story, Liz and Sarabeth, who are childhood friends, are emotionally distanced by Liz's teenage daughter's suicidal depression and the memories this conjures up for Sarabeth of her own mother's suicide. When Sarabeth retreats, we realize that a bad series of events can be devastating to a long-standing friendship, and not everyone is equipped to handle her friend's sadness or trauma. During these trying times, we see how a friendship can be weakened or strengthened. A past history, hopefully, in enough cases, can help the friends buoy each other.

Illusion versus Reality

Some friendships that appear unlikely end up being the most commanding of all. In the 2008 feature film *Baby Mama*, Tina Fey plays Kate Holbrook, a successful single working woman, and Amy Poehler plays Angie Ostrowiski, a working-class woman from South Philadelphia. When Kate discovers that she cannot carry a baby, she hires Angie to be her surrogate. The two women, with very different backgrounds and objectives, end up forming a true friendship. Another happy result is found in the novel *The Jane Austen Book Club* by Karen Joy Fowler. This story explores the ways in which five women of varying ages and at different stages in their lives, and one young man, meet to talk about Jane Austen's work. It is the friendship provided by the book club that helps each woman come to her personal epiphany. And so, a friendship that to outsiders might not seem plausible can supply each woman with a way to realize what she wants in life. What struck me as meaningful and touching in terms of long-standing friendships is what Barbara Walters wrote in her memoir, *Audition*, of her dear friend, Joan Rosen Marks. Ms. Walters told us that after some competition in their early days as classmates at Sarah Lawrence, they have been "friends for life."

Elizabeth Mazur points out in her study "Predicting Gender Differences in Same-Sex Friendships from Affiliation Motive and Value" that "structured" friendships consist of getting together for a specific cause, perhaps being on the same team, and bringing people together for a purpose, as described in the *Jane Austen Book Club*. The other format is an "unstructured" friendship, where friends meet solely for the purpose of "catching up on each other's lives." What Mazur found is that men are more likely to engage in structured situations and women in unstructured ones. As Lynn Harris wrote in "The 6 Must-Have Friends" in *Ladies' Home Journal* (LHJ.com), "it's crucial to have a colorful assortment of friends—from comfy to professional—to match the varied parts of your life."

Seeking Perfection

For Reilly, 24, who works in customer service on Long Island, her perception is that her friends are genuine and that she herself has sacrificer tendencies.

I'm very caring, and I'm the shoulder to lean on. People can count on me. My friends are similar to me, with a twist. They're more adventurous and I'm more introverted, and more willing to give of myself. I stand by a friend when she's being impossible or when things aren't going well—it's the right thing to do. Most of my friends are like me; we're African-American and come from the same background, and this is a common bond. Our mothers are from the islands and they always told us to do something with our lives. We all work at good jobs, and we spend time together.

When I didn't like this friend's boyfriend, I tried to be behind it, for her sake. It's how we were raised—to be a good friend and to make time for each other. After a while, I admit, I not only got sick of this friend's boyfriend, but I resented that she wasn't around anymore. Maybe I was jealous that she had a boyfriend. In the end,

I decided to stay friends with her. So what if things were changing for both of us, me with my work and the friend with this guy? We should be friends, if it's for real, even if we're in different places, even if it's not ideal. It matters.

Hitting the Road

Betty, 46, who is a nurse practitioner and lives in a Southern city, has more rules than Reilly and refuses to suffer an unhappy friendship.

I make it easy by not having many friends. If someone doesn't live up to my standards, I cut her out. I had one friend who made a mistake with work and that was it; as close as we were, it was over. You can't cross me, but that doesn't mean I'm not a real friend, or someone you can confide in. I am, and I'm a good listener. But I've had friends who didn't mean what they said and would do something against me. At first I was fooled; I didn't get it. Then I caught on and there wasn't any trust. Now that I'm older, I know to avoid this kind of friend, or someone who uses you. I am willing to be there for the right kind of friend, and I'm lucky to have a few of those. My mother always told me you can't count on many friends and it's better to have a few good ones and the rest acquaintances. I've taught my girls the same thing. I've warned them to be careful and to also work on having a few close girlfriends.

Although Reilly admitted to being jealous of her friend who is involved with a man, she remains loyal to her friend, while Betty views herself as the authentic friend who will not indulge any breach. What this shows us is that if a friendship fails, it is painful for both parties. The majority of women in my pool of interviewees reported that when they were more compromising and open-minded, they were better positioned for their goal, that of a thriving friendship.

Unrelenting Issues versus Support

Women who were able to get past the barriers reported a heightened awareness when it came to managing their friendships. The following strategies help.

Know What to Expect from the Relationship

Full disclosure as women become close is a way to avoid misunderstandings that lead to fall-outs. Yet over 50 percent of the women I interviewed were uncertain of what they expected in a close female friendship.

Avoid Rivalry

Rivalry is divisive and festers, especially if women do not discuss it. At the same time, it is unlikely that women would talk about feeling envious or jealous of a friend because as "good girls," we are not supposed to feel this way, especially toward a friend.

Get Beyond the Superficial

In the chapters on frenemies, trophy friends, users, and, in some instances, leaders, we have read about women who place an emphasis on lifestyle, labels, and status. Although these relationships can serve a purpose, ultimately they are not the stuff of authentic friendships.

Recommend Intervention for an Addiction or a Serious Problem

As mentioned earlier in this chapter, being honest is not always the easiest path. This, unfortunately, applies to a friend in need, when becoming involved might threaten the friendship. Nonetheless, in these cases, helping the friend is the genuine test.

Be a Solid Friend

Again, women say that being a truly good friend requires a conscious effort on some level. There are types of friends who lend themselves to this and are naturally better at it, more thoughtful, more flexible, and more generous, than others. But for any category of friend, there are times when we fall short; the bottom line is that friendships, like romances and mothering, require constancy, energy, and awareness.

Be Willing to Let the Wrong Friend Go

There are instances when anyone short of a frenemy, including an aggressive leader, a trophy friend, a misery lover, or a user, works in your life. Yet there are periods when they only create a toxic environment. At this point, whatever you get from the relationship is outweighed by the negative and you should sever the connection.

Kinship: Ages and Rituals

Nurturing our friendships is a concept women honor, although they aren't always able to put it into effect. For this reason, an all-female vacation, the kind we hear other women talking about but that not enough of us have taken ourselves, sounds almost dreamy. As Paula Span wrote in her article in *Good Housekeeping,* "The All-Girl Getaway," "making time for pals— real time—isn't just an indulgence. Experts say that intimate friendships can help women increase their sense of self-worth." Lianne, 43, who has two children and lives in a suburb, described her weekend with her female friends at a spa.

> My friends and I laughed and bonded—it reminded me of a slumber party. I don't know why it took me so long to make this time for my friends, but now we'll keep it up. My mother does it with her friends, and she swears by it. I should have started this years ago.

It becomes apparent in these profound friendships that self-disclosure, the desire to tell all of our personal desires, hopes, and actions to a friend, is a mechanism to draw in the other person. When the friendship is not on a par, women say they feel trapped and anxious if they reveal themselves and are watched too closely. Yet with the authentic friend, baring one's soul is satisfying. For those of us raised on *Anne of Green Gables,* there was Anne and her best friend in Avonlea, Diana Barry. These "best friends forever" endured a painful separation imposed by Diana's mother. A haunting picture of female friendship is shown to us in the film *Beaches,* starring Barbara Hershey, who plays Hillary, and Bette Midler, who plays CC.

As childhood friends from different worlds, they remain loyal to each other through divorce, illness, and death. In this sad tale, Hershey's character becomes terminally ill and chooses her best friend, CC, to be the guardian of her small daughter.

In *Thelma and Louise,* starring Geena Davis and Susan Sarandon, the concept of the authentic friend is taken to the limit. After being on the lam, the two friends decide to die for each other rather than surrender to the authorities, who they doubt will understand their distinctly female predicament. Dire circumstances are also at the center of the foreign film *4 Months, 3 Weeks and 2 Days.* In this film, a young college student, Otilia, helps her friend and roommate, Gabita, to procure an abortion in Ceauşescu's Romania in 1987, when the procedure was illegal and could prove fatal. The risks that Otilia takes in order to secure the plan for her friend, and the secrecy and danger surrounding every move, prove beyond a shadow of a doubt her level of commitment and the credibility of their friendship.

What Would I Do Without My Girlfriends?

Although an authentic friend may prove inadequate at times, it is the overall picture, the broad sweep of the canvas, that keeps women there. In our multilayered world filled with myriad obligations, including those of family, friends, motherhood, romance, work, adult siblings, and elderly parents, this friend is the keeper. The friends who can distract us from the burdens of life, and are sincere about their level of obligation, win the day.

While enormous energy is given to the authentic friend and to the dividends of the relationship, interestingly enough, not everyone searches for this. As research conveys, your own sense of self is reflected in the energy you give to your friends; genuine caring is an imperative, and the individual rapport is of great importance. Fifteen percent of my interviewees expressed that the "authentic friend" was almost an encumbrance, while 20 percent of the interviewees believed that the leader, the user, and the trophy friend had a more expedient place in their lives; they also spoke of not sticking it out with a disappointing friend. For the 65 percent who did *not* feel burdened by the relationship, their hopes were high when it came to this category of friend; they were in search of what the authentic friend offers.

Faithfulness at a Premium

After listening to a variety of stories for this chapter, I came to see clearly that the authentic friend soothes and comforts us.

Are you attached to your friend due to your history?
If you and your authentic friend base the friendship on a shared past and this works, that's fine. If you find it is the only link, you might try forging new ground, since you have a foundation already.

Would you feel deprived without this friend in your life?
Some women described feeling dependent upon their authentic friend, knowing she is the friend to count on. When the authentic friend is part mirroring friend or sharer, there are great perks in the relationship. Still, it's best to maintain your independence and not lean on this friend just because you can.

Are you committed to preserving the friendship through the hurdles?

What separates the authentic friend from the others is the level of commitment and trust, the promise that you are there in good times and bad. If this isn't a part of the equation, it isn't that echelon of friendship after all.

Are you able to grow personally within the relationship and respect each other's styles?

In a woman's life, at any age, happiness is at a premium. Those women who described a comfort level with their authentic friend *and* within themselves achieved this joy. They knew they were in the right place, reeling in the psychic rewards of their endeavors.

- -

Spinning Friends for a Lifetime

As I listened to the women profiled in this book and investigated studies on women's friendship, I realized the depth and breadth that this connection plays in a woman's life. The advent of the Internet, blogging, instant messaging, and cell phones creates more opportunity to stay in touch with a friend and more chances to find fault. Not only can we immediately contact someone, but we can also be critical when she isn't responsive, and vent in myriad ways that did not exist as recently as ten years ago. Yet many of the issues at the heart of the matter among women friends, those of trust, dependability, loyalty, reciprocity, and stability, go beyond the art of high tech and are emotional components of this female connection.

For the friends who are able to actualize the positive parts of the relationship and understand the negative aspects, there was an emphasis placed on being more accepting of each other. Amber, 33, who works in a pet shop and is a part-time graduate student, seeks out only healthy friendships.

I think now that I can sift through certain experiences. My friends are extroverted, because I'm that way. I treat a friend the way I want to be treated. I understand the friend who doesn't call back—I'm in a more forgiving mood; maybe I'm just happier with myself. I started this girlfriend bit when I was in kindergarten, so I've been doing it most of my life. There have been some unhappy occasions, and I've made some mistakes along the way. The worst was last winter when I got friendly with two girls who worked with me and they were mean and nasty. They were after me, I swear, as if they were playing some game. At first it didn't seem that way, but they were and I really suffered. I trusted them, I was so stupid, and I found out that you can't just do that. So they aren't my friends anymore and it was my choice, not theirs. The good news is that I get it, and ever since this happened, I can spot someone who will be a real friend and the person who won't be.

Patsy, 42, who lives in Southern California, where she teaches high school, recalled how a friend betrayed her in an age-old scenario—over a man. Like Amber, she made the decision to break free.

A two-faced former friend stole my boyfriend. The worst part was that she knew all about him through me—I had told her everything. Then she had to have him, and I thought she was very wrong. Her explanation, that it "just happened," didn't sit well with me. I was surprised, dumbfounded, when she insisted we could still be friends. Maybe she thought we were still in high school, where you had to suck up to the friend who wasn't a friend, who did this sort of thing. And it isn't much different from high school or college, which made it worse. It was a low blow, and I'm too old for this. I am fairly open with my friends, and I expect us to support one another. That's why she's a former friend now.

Unlike Amber or Patsy in her experience is Christina, 49, who is single and works in a laboratory in Pennsylvania.

I've been through a terrible divorce and I know the friends who count. The ones who are glad for me now that things are okay, those are my friends. The ones who liked it best when we were trading sob stories and I was always the most sympathetic (and the biggest loser), I stay away from today. It's weird that these women are mean to me now that I'm okay. Why would anyone begrudge me at this point? I wouldn't do that to a friend. I'd be happy that they're happy. As I've gotten older, I've wised up as to who is a real friend and who is there for some reason of her own. I never thought that anything as serious as a divorce or death was necessary to know who your real friends are, but now I know. I know that some women are too worried about themselves to be your friend when you become a single woman. Other women are threatened, and others think you have some kind of disease that they'll catch. It doesn't matter anymore why someone didn't stay my friend; I just know it's not the real thing, and that's what I'm looking for.

A Sisterhood in Flux

Although the three interviewees above are on separate courses, Amber as a mirroring friend, Patsy as a sharer, and Christina as a doormat, what they have in common is an awareness of how they fit with their friends and what the relationships provide or do not provide, for them. We do not question why both Patsy and Amber decided to cut out friends who were far from true blue, but in these instances, we are reminded of the importance of a "sisterhood." *Merriam-Webster's Collegiate Dictionary* defines *sisterhood* as "the solidarity of women based on shared conditions, experiences, or concerns" and defines a friend as "one attached to another by affection or esteem." These precepts are complex for women and have tremendous potential.

The key is to establish healthy ways to interact with women friends so that instead of feeling tied to the person, you feel there is a shared benefit. Just as the media has shown us the complications of female friendships, which I have referenced throughout this book, successful connections are exhibited as well. This includes in the long-standing television series *Friends*, where characters portrayed by Jennifer Aniston, Courtney Cox Arquette, and Lisa Kudrow interact with respect and humor. The 2008 television series *Lipstick Jungle*, featuring Brooke Shields as Wendy, a studio head; Kim Raver as Nico, a magazine editor; and Lindsay Price as Victory, a designer, exhibits three women struggling with their private lives, careers, husbands or love interests, and motherhood, but always finding support in one another's company. *Side Order of Life,* the 2007 television series starring Marisa Coughlan as Jenny and Diana-Maria Riva as Vivy, her best friend, is about how the trials and tribulations of life affect dedicated friends.

In Patricia Volk's novel *To My Dearest Friends*, Nanny Wunderlich and Alice Vogel, two women in midlife, have little in common but their recently deceased friend, Bobbi. They are thrown together when named coexecutors of Bobbi's safe-deposit box, which houses a love letter. Together the two women work to solve the mystery of Bobbi's lover, and along the way, an authentic friendship evolves. Another affirming tale of midlife female friendship is the film *Bonneville,* a movie starring Kathy Bates, Joan Allen, and Jessica Lange about three friends who take Lange's character's deceased husband's ashes from Utah to California for the funeral. *AARP, The Magazine's* March/April 2008 issue quoted Joan Allen on what *Bonneville* stands for and the possibilities of female bonding. "Women friendships films can be tricky," said Allen. "This one does a nice job of showing some women who are just trying to have some fun together."

Female Friendships as a Journey

As I have observed, women actively seek friends in every capacity, despite that in our multilayered lives, it seems impossible to find a flawless relationship. To compound matters, as important as the relationship is, the female friend dovetails with other obligations. Not only are women pulled in all directions—relocation, work, marriage, family, divorce, stepfamilies—but the human condition itself is not flawless. Women report that the following qualities make the relationships productive:

Give and Take. Women most frequently complain about the inequality of friendship. While it is easier said than done to achieve a balance, they try very hard to be sensitive to this.

A Lack of Criticism. Finding fault with our friends, unless they have done something reprehensible, can be counterproductive. Positive reinforcement goes a long way.

Shared Experiences versus Individuality. It is encouraging to see oneself in one's friend and to have a common ground. It is also meaningful to differentiate and to have boundaries.

Prioritizing the Relationship. Women of all ages complain that they are last on the totem pole when it comes to their closest friends. This also shifts; one day it is your complaint, the next go-round it is your friend's. Putting forth an effort to make the friendship count, and not breaking plans unnecessarily, is a start.

Degrees of Approval and Commitment

Although women have more female friends over their life span than they do romantic partners, this is, in part, because the issues in these relationships are very real. The friends we stick with are often similar to ourselves; the visceral tie that women feel to their friends, which men do not encounter with their male friends, is organic. When it works with a difficult friend, wisdom, a sense of personal well-being, and confidence kick in, enabling us to be more flexible. As Becca, 21, who is a student who works in a research lab and lives in North Dakota, told me, in her "crowd," one is a party girl, the other is too negative, and the other is a killjoy. Yet she thinks that each is worth keeping for the "other parts."

I want to stay friends with this group, but I know it 's a bit of a mess. One of my friends is out very late and can get into trouble. My other friend is very depressed, and my third close friend sees danger everywhere and is no fun. I want new friends, but we all are in college together and this is our last year. We live in the same house and we don't hang with other people. Some days it's okay; other days I think I need more friends. Part of the problem is how well we know one another, and how as long as we have this, why should we find new friends? I will make new friends at work when we graduate or if I move somewhere else. But these friends are the ones I count on, and I know what they'll do or won't do. I am sort of trapped, but I'm also sort of safe.

The Impact of Early Friendships

Becca enters the fray early, wrestling with the intricacies of these bonds. Already she is making excuses and compromises while realizing the advantage of hanging on to one's friends. The friends we make early on have etched a place in our hearts. So while we tend to search for different experiences in friendship throughout our lives, we often define the new relationships by what occurred with the earlier friendships. In this way, the mirroring friendships tend to be pervasive, threaded with other categories of friends.

As Leigh, 50, who is between jobs with no children, and lives in Maryland, described it, her female friends have been of utmost importance to her for decades. She is, in terms of her reliability and her attachment to old friends, similar to Becca.

My women friends mean so much to me. I've always had this close circle of friends, and I depend on them. For me it's very emotional, and I can't get that kind of backup from my husband. It's true that I have some friends from high school and from when I lived out of state who are disappointing and who don't come through; I keep them because there's always something I get from these women. Plus we used to be the same—about work, money, and guys. I remember those days. I still care about their lives and I know they care about where I'm at. Then I have new friends and this works better because I'm more careful. I'm older now and I know what to look for. I wouldn't necessarily choose the old friends today, but I'll never give them up.

Consider Desiree, 38, who works as a consultant and lives in Missouri with her teenage child. She is committed to these relationships, but discerning as well.

I really care about my female friends. I have a best friend who has been this to me for decades. The main ingredient is that we have healthy boundaries and treat each other with respect. Being honest and being a good listener is why we're together, and my goal is to always support her. I'm not lonely or dependent, but friends matter to me, and I rely on them. What I have done over the years is to let go of a friend who kept me from growing, who kept me from being myself. I always look for women who aren't whiny and who won't bring me down. So I'm picky about whom I meet and whom I befriend.

Rating Ourselves

In the above interviews, the delicate balance of self-preservation is juxtaposed with dedicating oneself to the relationship. Although no one describes an absolute distinction, there is a sense of awareness of what friendship provides. And as I have noted, our self-esteem is at the core of whom we choose for our closest friends. Dr. Ronnie Burak reminds us, "If you don't feel good about yourself, you won't pick a friend who you think is really terrific because you don't feel you deserve her. If you consider yourself a 'two,' then you won't be with a friend who is a 'ten.'"

The Female Condition: The Disturbance/Bliss Ratio

Regardless of the inherent ups and downs of friendship, women remain hopeful and tenacious. Thus, it is up to us to balance the portfolio, drawing a line when negativity surrounds the relationship.

Why is it so difficult to face disappointment in friendship?

We have to be honest with ourselves when we are not getting what we need from a relationship. You and your friend may be mismatched or may have grown apart despite efforts to hold the relationship together. This applies to women of any age, and can evoke guilt and negative behavior (not returning phone calls, not inviting the friend to events, not answering e-mails). Making excuses is often easier than leveling with the friend, but strained relations ultimately cause a rift. Close to 70 percent of women prefer that these relationships work out and, to this end, will deal with the friend in her sphere to maintain a semblance of rapport. For example, if your friend will go to a movie with you or out for dinner, but will not help paint your apartment, only count on her for what she can deliver.

Is there a new style of friendship in the twenty-first century?

It is striking how the modern female friendship has many elements of female friendship of centuries past, combined with the societal proscriptions of our present times. Older women describe their friends as guarded, boomers and Generation Xers say they share too much information with their friends, while some Generation Y and millennial women today have observed that their friends can be inaccessible. Other young women are bloggers, spilling their lives and feelings across the Internet, providing more information than is imaginable. And yet another flavor of woman has now appeared on the horizon, the friend who discards the sentimental factor and emotional side. As Theresa O'Rourke wrote in her article "I, Fembot," in the August 2007 issue of *Marie Claire*, "touchy-feely friendships" among women are being replaced by "a new breed of steely female(s)," the "fembots." O'Rourke described them as "a new kind of women," who do not elaborate on their feelings. The fembot is unfriendly, icy, and emotionally elusive—a reaction to overly emotional nineties friends, who, according to O'Rourke, are self-indulgent.

When do we stay despite less-than-optimal conditions?

Women frequently stay with a friend out of gratitude for her help during a trying period regarding finances, health, children, and/or divorce. The thankfulness trumps the missing parts, and loyalty hovers over the relationship. This applies to friends who have drifted apart as their lives change, friends who have had a falling-out in the past and are reunited, and those who recognize the inequalities in lifestyle or values but still feel an emotional tie. If a friend changes and you still make a conscious effort to be a part of her life, it is important to be aware of your frustrations, and perhaps hers. In this way, there is a heightened sense of the compromises made to keep the friendship intact.

When do we leave a friend?

When friends are too demanding, too compulsive, or self-destructive, or when you feel that you are losing yourself in the process, it is wise to make a break. If a friend has crossed you, or used you, or has become a "frenemy," then you ought to reconsider why you are involved. Although over 30 percent of my interviewees admitted to "breaking up" with a woman friend because it was a failed relationship, 50 percent considered a breakup without acting on it. The fact that this remains so difficult for women to do is a reflection of (a) the "good girl syndrome"—we are raised to not hurt someone's feelings, (b) our mother's influence, and (c) our deep attachment to the friend. Nonetheless, when the friend drains you, and the premise of the relationship is unhealthy or the connection requires too much work, letting go becomes the solution.

Bringing It Home

Of course, part of the kind of friend a woman is depends on her personality, combined with cultural influences and her individual experience.

From the beginning of my research for this book, I knew the prominence placed on friendship among women was consequential and the loss of a friend devastating. What I had not anticipated was the number of ways in which female friendships are both disturbing and enriching to the parties involved

and the degree of anticipation. Among the women I interviewed,

- ✗ A third had "ditched" a trying relationship, usually
  after a few dramatic events had injured the parties
  to the core.
- ✗ A third had remained, frustrated but committed, ready
  to make excuses, and willing to "tough out" a difficult
  friendship.
- ✗ The last third remained, believing that the friendship was fulfilling, or if it had deficiencies, improve-
  ment was possible and a change was in the future,
  thus the friends were "keepers."

The personal standard is higher today among women friends
than ever before, at a time in our country when women aspire
to equality, recognition, and opportunity. In the midst of our
accelerated schedules and the demands placed upon modern
woman is a longing for the best women friends. It is because
our lives are intricately woven that this need is so strident; the
investment in our female friends is in hope that these connections will nurture us, guide us, and offer us a safe haven. The
pros and cons of these relationships are a force to reckon with;
how we depend upon one another cranks up disappointment,
fantasies, and fractures among women. The relationships also
enable women to feel secure, appreciated, and admired. While
we can't escape the perils and problems of certain friendships,
those that are solid, soulful, and caring provide shelter from the
storm; they stand as testimony to the power of female bonds.

REFERENCES

AARP, The Magazine. March/April 2008.

Alleyne, Richard. "Cherie Is Hypocritical and Naive, Says Aide." *Telgraph. co.uk*, April 19, 2008.

Altman, Irwin, and Dalmas A. Taylor. *Social Penetration: The Development of Interpersonal Relationships.* New York: Holt, Rinehart & Winston, 1973.

American Heritage Dictionary.

Archie Comics. Created by Bob Montana in 1941.

Atwood, Margaret. *Cat's Eye.* New York: Anchor, 1998.

Austen, Jane. 1815. *Emma.* Repr., New York: Modern Library, 2001.

———. 1817. *Northanger Abbey.* Repr., New York: Barnes and Noble Classics, 2003.

Baby Mama. Directed by Michael McCullers. Universal Pictures, 2008.

Baker, Jean. *Mary Todd Lincoln: A Biography.* New York: W. W. Norton, 1989.

Ball, Aimee Lee. "The New and Improved Self-Esteem." *O, the Oprah Magazine*, January 2008.

Barash, Susan Shapiro. *Little White Lies, Deep Dark Secrets: The Truth About Why Women Lie.* New York: St. Martin's Press, 2008.

———. *Mothers-in-Law and Daughters-in-Law: Love, Hate, Rivalry and Reconciliation.* Far Hills, N.J.: New Horizon Press, 2001.

———. *Tripping the Prom Queen: The Truth About Women and Rivalry.* New York: St. Martin's Press, 2006.

Beaches. Directed by Garry Marshall. Buena Vista, 1988.

Belkin, Lisa. "It's Not the Job I Despise, It's You." *New York Times*, February 7, 2008.

Big Chill, The. Directed by Lawrence Kasdan. Columbia Pictures, 1983.

Big Love. Created by Mark V. Olsen et al. HBO, 2006–.

Blue Crush. Directed by John Stockwell. Imagine Entertainment, 2002.

Bond, M. H., and T. S. Cheung. "College Students' Spontaneous Self-Concept: The Effect of Culture Among Respondents in Hong Kong, Japan, and the United States." *Journal of Cross-Cultural Psychology,* Vol. 14, No. 2 (1983), pp. 153–71.

Bonneville. Directed by Christopher N. Rowley. SenArt Films, 2006.

Boon, S. D. "Dispelling Doubt and Uncertainty: Trust in Romantic Relationships." In *Dynamics of Relationships,* Vol. 4: *Understanding Relationship Processes,* ed. S. Duck. Thousand Oaks, CA: Sage Publications, 1994.

Borysenko, Joan. *A Women's Book of Life: The Biology, Psychology, and Spirituality of the Feminine Life Cycle.* New York: Riverhead, 1998.

Break-Up, The. Directed by Peyton Reed. Universal Pictures, 2006.

Brookner, Anita. *The Rules of Engagement.* New York: Vintage, 2005.

Buss, David M. "Evolutionary Psychology: A New Paradigm for Psychological Science." *Psychological Inquiry,* Vol. 6, No. 1 (1995), pp. 1–30.

Cama Adentro (Live-in Maid). Directed by Jorge Gaggero. Aquafilms, 2004.

Carey, Benedict. "You Remind Me of Me." *New York Times,* February 12, 2008.

Cheng, C., M. H. Bond, and S. C. Chan. "The Perception of Ideal Best Friends by Chinese Adolescents." *International Journal of Psychology,* Vol. 30, No. 1 (1995), pp. 91–108.

Clueless. Directed by Amy Heckerling. Paramount Pictures, 1995.

Conroy, Pat. *The Prince of Tides.* New York: Dial Press, 2002.

Cunningham, M. R., and A. P. Barbee. "Social Support." In *Close Relationships: A Sourcebook,* eds. C. Hendrick and S. S. Hendrick, 273–285. Thousand Oaks, Calif.: SAGE Publications.

DeDonato, Colette. "An Open and Shut Marriage." *New York Times,* February 3, 2008.

Desperate Housewives. Created by Marc Cherry. ABC Network, 2004–.

Dick Cavett Show, The (talk show), June 21, 1979.

Drew, Carla. "My Turn: A Sisterhood of Suffering." *Newsweek,* March 31, 2008.

Enchanted. Directed by Kevin Lima. Walt Disney Studios, 2007.

Flagg, Fannie. *Fried Green Tomatoes at the Whistle Stop Café.* New York: Ballantine, 1997.

4 Months, 3 Weeks and 2 Days. Directed by Cristian Mungiu. BAC Films, 2007.

Fowler, Karen Joy. *The Jane Austen Book Club*. New York: Putnam, 2004.

Frazier, Charles. *Cold Mountain: A Novel*. New York: Vintage, 1998.

Fried Green Tomatoes. Directed by Jon Avnet. Universal Pictures, 1991.

Friedman, Richard A., MD. "About That Mean Streak of Yours: Psychiatry Can Do Only So Much." *New York Times*, February 6, 2007.

Friends. Created by David Crane and Marta Kauffman. NBC Network, 1994–2004.

Friends with Money. Directed by Nicole Holofcener. This Is That Productions, 2006.

Garmezy, Norman, and Michael Rulter. *Stress, Coping, and Development in Children*. New York: McGraw-Hill, 1983.

Girls Next Door, The. Created by Kevin Burns and Hugh Hefner. E! Channel, 2005–.

Golden Girls, The. Created by Susan Harris. NBC Network, 1985–1992.

Gossip Girl. Developed by Josh Schwartz and Stephanie Savage. The CW Network, 2007–.

Grifters, The. Directed by Stephen Frears. Cineplex-Odeon Films, 1990.

Harris, Lynn. "The 6 Must-Have Friends." *Ladies' Home Journal*. www.lhj.com, 2008.

Hauser, Brooke. "Fortune's Sisters." *New York Times*, January 6, 2008.

Hills, The. Created by Adam Divello. MTV, 2006–.

Honeymooners, The. Created by Jackie Gleason. Jackie Gleason Enterprises, 1955–1956.

Hornaday, Ann. "That Wonderful Woman! Oh, How I Loathe Her. The Tricky Emotion Between Idolizing and Despising." *Washington Post*, February 22, 2006.

Huffstutter, P. J. "Frontier Justice in an Online World?" *Seattle Times*, November 23, 2007.

I Love Lucy. Created by Lucille Ball. CBS Television, 1951–1957.

Johnson, H. Durell, et al. "Identity as a Moderator of Gender Difference in the Emotional Closeness of Emerging Adults' Same and Cross-Sex Friendships." *Adolescence*, Vol. 42, No. 165 (2007), pp. 1–23.

Jones, G. P., and M. H. Denbo. "Age and Sex Role Differences in Intimate Friendships During Childhood and Adolescence." *Merrill-Palmer Quarterly*, Vol. 35, No. 4 (1989), pp. 445–62.

Juno. Directed by Jason Reitman. Fox Searchlight Pictures, 2007.

Kaysen, Susanna. *Girl, Interrupted.* New York: Vintage, 1994.

Kearnes, Fara. "Paris Hilton and Nicole Richie Confirm Their Breakup." StarBlogs.net, April 20, 2005.

Kellerman, Barbara. *Followership: How Followers Are Creating Change and Changing Leaders.* Cambridge, Mass.: Harvard Business School Press, 2008.

Leblanc, Gabrielle. "Things Happy People Do." The Huffington Post, April 4, 2008.

Legally Blonde. Directed by Robert Luketic. 20th Century Fox, 2001.

Lipstick Jungle. Created by De Ann Heline and Eileen Heisler. NBC Network, 2008–.

Mad Money. Directed by Callie Khouri. Big City Pictures, 2008.

Malikiosi-Loizos, M., and L. L. Anderson. "Accessible Friendships, Inclusive Friendships, Reciprocated Friendships as Related to Social and Emotional Loneliness in Greece and the USA." *European Psychologist,* Vol. 4, No. 3 (1999), pp. 165–78.

Mary Tyler Moore Show, The. Created by James L. Brooks and Allan Burns. CBS Network, 1970–1977.

Mazur, Elizabeth. "Predicting Gender Differences in Same-Sex Friendships from Affiliation Motive and Value." *Psychology of Women Quarterly,* Vol. 13, No. 3. (1989), pp. 277–91.

Mean Girls. Directed by Mark S. Waters. Paramount Pictures, 2004.

Merriam Webster's Collegiate Dictionary, 10th ed. Springfield, Mass.: Merriam-Webster Incorporated, 1993.

Me Without You. Directed by Sandra Goldbacher. Fireworks Pictures, 2001.

Michael Clayton. Directed by Tony Gilroy. Warner Brothers, 2007.

Minot, Susan. *Evening.* New York: Knopf, 1998.

Montgomery, L. M. 1908. *Anne of Green Gables.* Repr., New York: Laurel Leaf, 1997.

Morry, M. M., and C. Harasymchuk. "Perceptions of Locus of Control and Satisfaction in Friendships: The Impact of Problem-Solving Strategies." *Journal of Social and Personal Relationships,* Vol. 22, No. 2 (2005), pp. 183–206.

Ninjawords Dictionary. http://ninjawords.com.

Notes on a Scandal. Directed by Richard Eyre. BBC Films, 2006.

Nottage, Lynn. *Intimate Apparel* (play), 2003.

Oswald, Debra L., Eddie M. Clark, and Cheryl M. Kelly. "Friendship Maintenance: An Analysis of Individual and Dyad Behaviors." *Jour-*

nal of Social and Clinical Psychology, Vol. 23, No. 3 (2004), pp. 413–41.

Packer, Ann. *Songs Without Words.* New York: Knopf, 2007.

Packer, ZZ, "The Finish Party," *O, The Oprah Magazine,* October 2007.

Paul, Marla. *The Friendship Crisis: Finding, Making, and Keeping Friends When You're Not a Kid Anymore.* New York: Rodale, 2004.

Perrotta, Tom. *The Abstinence Teacher.* New York: St. Martin's Press, 2007.

Pinker, Steven. "The Moral Instinct." *The New York Times Magazine,* January 13, 2008.

Prentice, Deborah A., Dale T. Miller, and Jennifer R. Lightdale. "Asymmetries in Attachments to Groups and to Their Members: Distinguishing Between Common-Identity and Common-Bond Groups." *Personality and Social Psychology Bulletin,* Vol. 20, No. 5 (1994), pp. 484–93.

Rich, Adrienne. *Of Women Born: Motherhood as Experience and Institution.* New York: W. W. Norton, 1995.

Rohter, Larry. "A Part Made for Her, About Life with a Maid." *New York Times,* July 15, 2007.

Rook, Karen. "Reciprocity of Social Exchange and Social Satisfaction Among Older Women." *Journal of Personality and Social Psychology,* No. 52 (1987), pp. 145–54.

Rosenbloom, Stephanie. "For Housewives, She's the Hot Ticket." *New York Times,* April 13, 2008.

———. "She's So Cool, So Smart, So Beautiful: Must Be a Girl Crush." *New York Times,* August 22, 2005

Rubin, Lillian. *Just Friends: The Role of Friendship in Our Lives.* New York: Harper Perennial, 1986.

Sales, Nancy Jo. "I'm with Her!" *Vanity Fair,* September 2007.

Savacool, Julia. "Interview with Star Jones Reynolds." *Marie Claire,* August 2007.

Schoeneman, Deborah. "Mermaids Past and Present Keep Things Real." *New York Times,* January 6, 2008.

Seeley, Elizabeth A., Wendi L. Gardner, Ginger Pennington, and Shira Gabriel. "Circle of Friends or Members of a Group? Sex Differences in Relational and Collective Attachment to Groups. *Group Processes and Intergroup Relations,* Vol. 6, No. 3 (2003), pp. 251–63.

Sex and the City (TV series). Created by Darren Star. Darren Star Productions, 1998–2004.

Sex and the City (movie). Directed by Michael Patrick King. Darren Star Productions, 2008.

Sholl, Jessie. "Friendship Too Tight for Breathing Room." *New York Times,* August 5, 2007.

Side Order of Life. Created by Margaret Nagle. Lifetime Television Networks, 2007.

Sidhwa, Bapsi. *Water: A Novel.* Minneapolis: Milkweed Editions, 2006.

Simmons, Rachel. *Odd Girl Out: The Hidden Culture of Agression in Girls.* New York: Harvest Books, 2003.

Simple Life, The. Created by the Fox Broadcasting Company. Fox Broadcasting Company, 2003–2005; E! Network, 2006–2007.

Single White Female. Directed by Barbet Schroeder. Columbia Pictures Corporation, 1992.

Solomon, Dorothy Allred. *The Sisterhood: Inside the Lives of Mormon Women.* New York: Palgrave Macmillan, 2008.

Span, Paula. "The All-Girl *Getaway.*" *Good Housekeeping,* June 1, 1999.

Steil, Janice M., Vanessa L. McGann, and Anne S. Kahn. "Entitlement. Encyclopedia of Women and Genders," Vol. 1. New York: Academic Press, 2001.

Steinke, Darcey. "The Exchange: Kindness for Rudeness." *New York Times,* December 23, 2007.

Sternberg, Robert J. "A Triangular Theory of Love." *Psychological Review,* Vol. 93., No. 2 (1986), pp. 119–35.

———. *The Triangle of Love: Intimacy, Passion, Commitment.* New York: Basic Books. 1988.

Swan Lake. Composed by Pyotr Tchaikovsky. 1876.

Taylor, Katherine. "Girls, Mean and Otherwise." *New York Times,* September 16, 2007.

Taylor, S. E., L. C. Klein, B. P. Lewis, T. L. Gruenewald, R. A. R. Gurung, and J. A. Updegraff, "Behavioral Responses to Stress: Tend-and-Befriend, Not Fight-or-Flight." *Psychological Review,* Vol. 107, No. 3 (2000), pp. 411–29.

Thelma & Louise. Directed by Ridley Scott. MGM Pictures, 1991.

27 Dresses. Directed by Anne Fletcher. Fox 200 Pictures, 2008.

U.S. Census. www.census. gov/index.html.

Valen, Kelly. "My Sorority Pledge? I Swore Off Sisterhood." *New York Times,* December 2, 2007.

Veniegas, R. C., and L. A. Peplau. "Power and the Quality of the Same-

Sex Friendships." *Psychology of Women Quarterly*, Vol. 21, No. 2 (1997), pp. 279–97.

Verbrugge, Lois M. "The Structure of Adult Friendship Choice." *Social Forces,* Vol. 56, No. 2, (1977), pp.

———. "Multiplexity in Adult Friendships." *Social Forces*, Vol. 57, No. 4 (1979).

Volk, Patricia. *To My Dearest Friends.* New York: Knopf, 2007.

Walls, Jeannette. "Does Locklear Blame Richards for Her Divorce? Msnbc .com, April 27, 2006.

Way, Niobe, and Melissa L. Greene. "Trajectories of Perceived Friendship Quality During Adolescence,."*Journal of Research on Adolescence*, Vol. 16, No. 4 (2006), pp. 589–92.

Weisberger, Lauren. *The Devil Wears Prada.* New York: Doubleday, 2003.

Wells, Rebecca. *Divine Secrets of the Ya-Ya Sisterhood.* New York: Harper Perennial, 1997.

Whitworth, Damian. "Oral History: The Monica Lewinsky Scandal Ten Years On." Times Online, January 15, 2008.

"Who Wore It Best?" *Us Weekly*, August 27, 2007.

Wilson, Eric G. *Against Happiness: In Praise of Melancholy.* New York: Farrar, Straus & Giroux, 2008.

Wiseman, Rosalind. *Queen Bees and Wannabes: Helping Your Daughter Survive Cliques, Gossip, Boyfriends, and Other Realities of Adolescence.* New York: Three Rivers Press, 2003.

Wizard of Oz, The. Directed by Victor Fleming. MGM Pictures, 1939.

Women, The. Directed by George Kukor. MGM,1939.

Women, The. Directed by Diane English. Jagged Pictures, 2008.

Wright, P. H. "Men's Friendships, Women's Friendships, and the Alleged Inferiority of the Latter." *Sex Roles*, Vol. 8, No. 1 (1982), pp. 1–20.

ACKNOWLEDGMENTS

I owe a great debt to the women who revealed their experiences, fears, and hopes with their female friends. Their stories are at the heart of the matter.

Jennifer Enderlin, my amazing editor, planted the seeds, Meredith Bernstein cultivated this project, and Alice Martell expanded the horizon. Their knowledge has made all the difference.

In alphabetical order: At St. Martin's Press: Meg Drislane, Rachel Ekstrom, Courtney Fischer, Sara Goodman, John Murphy, Sally Richardson, Matthew Shear, Dori Weintraub. For listening: Lori Ames, Brondi Borer, Tina Chen, Gail Clott, Ashley Deiser, Susie Finesman, Brit Geiger, Cindy Land, Meryl Moss, Judy Shapiro, Cynthia Vartan. Jennie Ripps, my muse, Robert Marcus, my loyal attorney, Susanna LaBarre, Amanda Soule, and Jessica Soule for their assistance. In academia: Carol Camper, Lewis Burke Frumkes, David Linton, Magda Maczynska at Marymount Manhattan College, Suzanne M. Murphy at Teachers College, Columbia University. In Hollywood: Jon Avnet, Nancy Bennetts, Howard Braunstein, Charles Busch, Michael Jaffe, Deb Newmyer, Sally Robinson, Bruce Vinokour, Meredith Wagner, Allison Wallach, Ellyn Williams. The professionals who have contributed their thoughts to this book: Dr. Ronnie Burak, Dr. Donald

Cohen, Dr. Barton Goldsmith, Dr. Claire Owen, Seth Shulman. My mother, Selma Shapiro, best critic and staunchest supporter, and my father, Herbert L. Shapiro, savvy researcher, my in-laws, Helene and Ted Barash, and truest friends.

Jennie, Michael, and Elizabeth Ripps, my treasured children. Finally, Gary A. Barash, my wise, patient husband (and walking thesaurus).

Readers' Guide

Questions for Discussion for *Toxic Friends:*
The Antidote for Women Stuck in Complicated Friendships

1. The author describes ten different kinds of friends and how we interact with each type. What types do you identify with the most and why?
2. The author starts out by telling us that one of the greatest truths is that losing a female friend can have as many repercussions as breaking up with a boyfriend or husband. Would you agree with this, and have you had an experience like this?
3. Would you consider yourself someone who "romanticizes" her female friends? Or are you a pragmatist, who sees her friends for who they truly are?
4. What is the author's definition of female friendship, and how does it fit into one's everyday life in terms of work, children, and romance? Do you think there's a way to improve how your friend is positioned?
5. Discuss being open and truthful with a friend and why this is oftentimes a struggle. How much disclosure and how much intimacy do you feel you need with your female friends?
6. The author suggests that women lower their expectations in order for their female friendships to improve. How would this work as a guiding principle for your?
7. When it comes to envy and jealousy among friends, do you feel that this occurs often in your relationships? Have you ever been surprised about how this has evolved in a close friendship?
8. The author describes various scenarios, including a friendship with a leader, a doormat, a sacrificer, a user, a frenemy,

and a sharer. Among these kind of friends, what causes the most friction between you and the friend? Do you think age and stage of life has anything to do with it?

9. The author explores betrayal and manipulation among female friends and suggests when it's time to end the relationship as well as the possibilities for salvaging the relationship. What has occurred within your own friendships where you've decided to call it quits, and when have you toughed it out and why?

10. Define the author's take on the mirroring friend. What do you find to be the trickiest aspect of such a friendship, and how do you deal with eventually not being in the same circumstances as this friend?

11. The author believes that being comfortable with yourself in the relationship is key to a successful friendship, but also finds that for many women, this is complicated. Honesty is a big part of this, and women struggle to be honest. How does this apply to you?

12. What are your thoughts about the author's advice on facing our disappointments in our friends, and compromising and/ or healing in order to preserve the friendship, rather than let it go? What are your boundaries and where do you draw the line?

13. Are there parts of the book that you would recommend that provide a way to work through issues with your female friends?

14. What have you learned by reading this book? Is there any chapter that has given you insights and offers an "aha" moment? What did you find most useful about her study?

15. The author believes that mothers have influence over their daughters in terms of female rivalry, based on their own experience. Essentially, mothers teach their daughters what to do or not do with their female friends. Do you find this useful and insightful?